PAST LIFE THERAPY

D1240547

IN THE SAME SERIES:

THORSONS
PRINCIPLES
OF

PAST LIFE
THERAPY

JUDY HALL

Thorsons
An Imprint of HarperCollins*Publishers*

Thorsons
An Imprint of HarperCollins*Publishers*
77–85 Fulham Palace Road,
Hammersmith, London W6 8JB
1160 Battery Street
San Francisco, California 94111–1213

Published by Thorsons 1996

3 5 7 9 10 8 6 4 2

A catalogue record for this book
is available from the British Library

ISBN 0 7225 3353 5

Printed and bound in Great Britain by
Caledonian International Book Manufacturing Ltd, Glasgow

CONTENTS

ACKNOWLEDGEMENTS

I would like to thank Dave Gilbert for all his assistance with hypnotherapy – and for much else besides. Also Diana Keel and Bernadette Jaye of the College of Past Life Healing gave freely of their time and knowledge. My thanks to them and to all the people who gave permission for their case histories to be used in this book.

INTRODUCTION

INTO THE PAST

D o you believe you have lived before? Many people do. Do you wonder if you might have? You are not alone. More and more people are opening up to the intriguing prospect of having previously lived, and died. An increasing number seek aid in 'going back to other lives'. They may simply want to explore the possibility that they have lived before, they may be looking for evidence of past lives, or they may have a more pressing reason for wanting to know what happened to them. In a recent poll, a surprising 49 per cent of people in southern Britain said they believed they might have lived before. In parts of the USA the figure is no doubt higher. In the East, almost everyone believes in reincarnation.

Reincarnation is the belief that, having inhabited a different body, in another time and possibly another place, and having then died, someone returns again to earth in a new body, in other words reincarnates. Knowledge of past lives may be accessed through spontaneous visions, flashbacks, dreams, or déjà vu; or it can be induced through hypnosis and other techniques.

A flashback is a spontaneous vision of, or a remembering of, a past-life experience. It may come out of the blue or be triggered by a place or a person, or by touching the part of the body where the memory is stored, or it may surface during meditation. Flashbacks may be experienced by more than one person, either at the same time or on different occasions. Such spontaneous memories may have started in childhood and carried through to adult life, as in the case of Jenny Cockell.

Yesterday's children: Jenny Cockell

Throughout her childhood, Jenny Cockell had dreams and flashbacks of living in another place. She drew sketch maps of her 'other home'. Over the years she gathered an enormous amount of material. She was convinced that she had been a mother tragically separated from her children by an early death with terrible consequences for those children. She was determined to find them again.

Though she is English in her present life, Jenny Cockell's search led her to Ireland and to a moving reunion with 'her children', who by now are much older than her. Her 'son' said that, whilst not totally convinced about reincarnation (he had been a Catholic all his life), Jenny Cockell had knowledge about his family that only his mother could have. Events had taken place exactly as she recalled them. The house was as she had drawn it all those years ago. The family had been split up following her death, which had been traumatic.

Many celebrities believe in reincarnation. Richard Gere, Tina Turner, Shirley MacLaine and a former Chief Constable of Manchester are just a few of those who have spoken publicly about their belief. General Patton, a Second World War hero, believed he had been both Hannibal and Alexander the Great in addition to several other lesser figures on the war stage of history. Interestingly enough, Alexander himself was a great believer in reincarnation, as was Plato. The Spanish painter

Salvador Dali remembered life as Saint John of the Cross. Napoleon Bonaparte was convinced that he was the reincarnation of Charlemagne, head of the Holy Roman Empire. Henry Ford and Benjamin Franklin were both firm believers.

Having lived before implies a continuity of consciousness: the continuous existence of the human soul. After all, if you have lived and died before, the implication is that you will do so again ... and again. This may well explain the imperative urge to 'prove it' that many people have. An urge that is now being catered for by television and magazines.

Actress Paula Hamilton was hypnotically regressed to a former life as a man, Ashley Brown, for a British TV programme. When questioned, Ashley gave his name and details of his family, including an address in London. He said he had sailed to Ireland from Parkgate, a little known, long disused port near Liverpool that once handled the bulk of Irish sailings. Paula Hamilton had never heard of the place, nor, in her present life, been to Ireland. In her former incarnation, Ashley ended up as a baker in Dublin, giving details such as the name of a (now vanished but verifiable from old maps) alley in which his shop was situated and the Protestant church close by in which he was married. He died of a lung disease due to ingested flour: a common cause of death in bakers of the period.

Hypnotic regression

Hypnosis is an altered state of consciousness during which previously inaccessible memories are accessed. In hypnotic regression, the subject is taken back, or regressed, to another lifetime. There are other methods of regression.

A researcher employed by the programme was able to verify many of the details in this obscure person's life, although it was not possible to actually prove Ashley's existence as many of the relevant Irish records have been destroyed. The researcher did find someone named Brown at the London Kensington address, who could well have been a relative, but of Ashley himself there was, unfortunately, no mention.

This is one of the difficulties. It is not easy to prove beyond doubt that the apparent memories and experiences of past lives mean that reincarnation is true. But this does not stop people trying. It occupies serious researchers, sometimes for years as with Professor Ian Stevenson. There is a popular magazine devoted to past life memories, and many people have a vested interest because they believe they were historical personages. Tina Turner, for instance, believes she was the Egyptian Pharaoh, Queen Hapshepshut. Unfortunately, even if the details gained under hypnosis are confirmed, it is almost impossible to prove that a person now living was that long-dead person. There are other possible explanations, as we shall see. Notwithstanding, experiences like those of Jenny Cockell are compelling reasons to believe. Especially for the recallee. It is usually the experience itself that convinces, not the 'evidence'. Paula Hamilton commented that what impressed her most was that, during her regression, she felt, and spoke, as a man would.

There is, however, another reason for exploring the past other than simply curiosity or a desire to prove the truth of reincarnation. This is that the key to the present can lie there. This is what past life therapy is all about. The value of past life therapy lies not in what it may prove about your former life, or lives, but in how it can enhance your present one. Past life therapists believe they can heal the past to change the present. Certainly, in my own practice, I have seen some dramatic improvements in health and well-being. Phobias dissolve, chronic diseases disappear, emotional disturbances heal, relationships improve. Nevertheless, it does not have to be dramatic, or traumatic either. Many people simply feel better able to handle their present life.

Past Life Therapy

Being guided to a time before birth in the present life, that is, into another life, to uncover and heal the causes of problems and difficulties that have arisen in the present life.

The sense of something suddenly clicking into place, of understanding the previously inexplicable, can throw light on many of our day-to-day feelings. A woman regressed to being a much loved only child. A real 'daddy's girl'. She was given a pony for her birthday and was ecstatically happy. She leapt onto the pony, which bolted. She was thrown and killed. Asked what connection this had with her present life, she replied that whenever she was happy she would start to worry. There was always a vague sense of dread. She associated being happy with fear and loss. Being killed in a moment of supreme happiness in that other life made sense of her fear.

In a similar way, another woman wanted to know why she had always felt so responsible for her sister and had a compulsion to rush to her side whenever she was unwell. As a young child, this had caused her great anguish when she was sent away to school on the other side of the world. As an adult of mature years, it created many inconvenient situations, continually disrupting her life. In the regression, she was a happy healthy child, with an invalid sister. It was her duty to stay with her sister, she was told, whenever she wanted to go out to play. Indeed, her sister would beg: "Don't leave me, promise me you will always be here." She was, not just in that life but in the present one too. Recognizing that fact allowed her to detach from the old, no longer applicable, promise.

The result of such an experience may not always be dramatic, but it can be. It may not always have physical repercussions, but it often does. The effect of a past life can be emotionally crippling. It may also explain a great deal about present life relationships.

My first solo regression was instigated by someone saying to a friend of mine: "I see you dressed as a nun." His method of regressing people was to 'tune in' to their past lives himself, and tell them what he saw. The person was then supposed to join in. It triggered a 'flashback' in her, but one she strenuously tried to block out. She immediately began to shake her head emphatically and to make a most distressed noise. Tears poured down her cheeks. As the 'regressor' was not looking at her, he did not at first notice what was happening. When he did, he simply said: "Oh, don't want to do it? Ok, I'll go" and did, leaving me with a woman still deeply distressed and violently shaking her head. The noise had risen to a crescendo and she was wringing her hands. Clearly something had to be done.

I took her through a difficult incarnation as a nun, one with no physical comfort at all and little spiritual sustenance. She had, apparently, been put into the convent to stop her marrying her great love, and she missed him every moment of her life. To her, love was something set aside and sacred. It had nothing to do with physical life. The regression was graphic: she had body lice and scratched at them continuously. Her clothes were heavy and uncomfortable and she pulled fitfully at them. Her hands and knees were raw from kneeling and scrubbing floors. On the rare occasion she took a bath, it was in cold water in her linen shift. She never saw herself naked. The body was anathema. Her hair had been hacked off by the mistress of the novices, and her scalp never healed properly. Interestingly enough, she commented: "And she bloody well did it in this life too." I had to return to that comment later as I felt it had great bearing on her life now.

The only way out of that life was to take her forward through death, but she was still wearing the robes in the between life state. She took them off and burnt them. She pictured having a bath to clear the lice and fleas. We grew her hair and used lotions on her skin. She dressed herself in silken clothes. Eventually she burnt the convent down, but she kept the chapel as she had found what little sustenance and comfort she had there. All the time her language grew stronger and bluer and she was not a person who ever swore. Indeed, in her present life she prided herself on never having lost control of herself, "in anger or in passion." Burning down the convent seemed to be a release for great feeling, of deep anger that had lain beneath the surface all through her present life.

I asked her about the 'she did it in this life too' comment. She explained that, as a 15 year old, she had gone out with a boy against her mother's wishes. Her enraged mother hacked off her waist-length blonde hair with shears, cutting into her scalp as she did so. Her mother, whom she hated in her present life, had been the mistress of novices in that past life. Her great love then was her great love now. But she had not married him. Her mother had broken up the relationship. However, they had continued to see each other every week for over forty years as they were "deeply in love". The dichotomy between 'sacred' and 'profane' love was strong in her. Her distaste for the body and 'things of the flesh' all too apparent. She had married someone merely to have children. When she had a child, the sex stopped and eventually the marriage broke down. She had never had sexual intercourse with the man she 'loved'. She said she did not know what it was to 'make love'. Her emotional life was frozen back in that previous life. Her difficult relationship with her mother certainly seemed to be a reflection of just how much she had hated that mistress of the novices. These were just some of the many correlations between that life and the present. Much reframing and releasing needed to be done.

The Between Life State

A state of non-physical being to which souls pass after death. It may be a bright light, a place, a colour or energy. Cultural and religious expectations influence the experience. People see what they expect to see: heaven, hell, paradise, Valhalla, or whatever. Conscious awareness and memory is retained and expanded here and an overview of all lives is possible: forwards or backwards. In some levels of the between life state, the soul may appear to be housed within a body, while in others it is non-corporeal. Healing and reframing can easily be carried out here and the effect carried forward into the present life.

Reframing

To reframe a past life experience involves changing the 'life script'. It may entail a change of scenario, replaying it with a different outcome. It may need to be seen from a different perspective. Changing the past in this way changes the present life experience.

That that 'regression' was precipitated by someone else and not carried through illustrates one of the pitfalls. Not everyone is prepared, or able, to deal with something that traumatic. They may activate it but not know how to handle it. I was fortunate in that I, as well as having a natural affinity with the work, had been in training with an expert who had over forty year's experience, and so I was able to pick up the pieces.

But!! It is difficult to ensure that all past life therapists are knowledgeable, experienced and properly trained. There are some gifted amateurs who simply fell into the work and found it came naturally, as I did. But most of us supplement that natural ability with other training. Many therapists come into past life therapy via other disciplines such as psychotherapy or hypnosis. But even then, extensive experience in the specific work of past life therapy is essential if the therapist is to be able to deal with everything that arises. Some hypnotherapists do not believe in past lives, and if they trigger one, they will not work with it.

There are several approaches. Techniques differ. The number of sessions required will vary. The approach you seek will depend on whether you simply want to explore other lives, or to deal with deep-seated problems. Some therapists merely re-run the past life. Others work at reframing and healing the root cause, utilizing a variety of therapeutic options. Which one will suit you depends on your reasons for seeking therapy in the first place.

Whatever your reason, prospective users of past life therapy should seek knowledgeable guidance and a reputable therapist. Personal recommendation is always a good start, but the right therapist for you is still very much an individual matter. Do not be afraid to ask questions before you book a session, or to go for an exploratory chat before a regression. You need to feel safe and well cared for by an experienced and empathetic professional. Such people do exist. This book will show you what to look out for, and your life may well change for the better as a result of meeting such a person.

WHAT IS PAST LIFE THERAPY?

Past life therapy is an holistic therapy, that is to say it works on the body, mind, emotions and spirit. It takes you back to before your birth, regresses you to another lifetime, to sort out difficulties you may be experiencing in the present. The reason for undertaking past life therapy is to improve your life, now. Its object is to make life easier, better and more fulfilling, in this present moment.

> ### Regression
>
> To re-experience or relive a former life as though it were happening now.

Past life therapy is based on the principle of cause and effect (also known as karma). What has been set in motion at some time in the past creates an effect on a person's physical, emotional, mental or spiritual well-being, now. This cause may be a desire, thought, feeling, emotion, vow, promise, decision, evasion or traumatic experience, amongst others. Very often, at a moment of trauma, a section of our consciousness (part of our overall self) detaches itself and remains 'stuck'. Past life causes may manifest in the present as a phobia, chronic illness or body state, addiction, mental disorder, inability to make relationships, inexplicable attraction or aversion to someone, recurring nightmares, or a simple sense of unease.

Karma

Karma means action. It is the principle of cause and effect. Taken simply it means that for every action there is a consequence. What has been put into motion in the past has effects in the present. Karma is, however, both subtle and complex. Thoughts and attitudes can create karma just as strongly as can tangible deeds and events. What we set in motion now, and our motivation, will influence our future. Karma is also the conditions our soul needs in order to grow spiritually, it is what we create for ourselves. Karma operates at different levels: personal, group/family/racial, collective and cosmic.

The other side of the coin is that particular skills, interests, likings, or for that matter passions in this life may well also be the result of past life experiences. Knowledge of these may help someone to handle their present life better, or point the way to an appropriate career choice, hobbies, etc.

So, as well as clearing blockages and old dis-ease, past life therapy can be used to trace relationship patterns and old connections, to reconnect to the purpose of incarnating, and to previous knowledge and skills. It can also look forward to 'future lives': what is still to come.

WHAT CAN IT DO?

Past life therapy can be helpful in many different areas: pho-bias, irrational fears, health problems; removing fear of death; understanding eating disorders, family dysfunction, addic-tions, sexual difficulties, marital and relationship problems. It defuses negative patterns, finding the reasons for present life difficulties, and setting positive change in motion.

It can change your life dramatically, eliminating guilt and anxiety. It will help you to develop your potential, unlock latent talents, create better understanding of others, reveal your life purpose and reason for incarnating, and initiate new patterns of response, not reaction. By rewriting your life script, you can remove outworn emotional and doctrinal conditioning, and attune to an inner source of knowledge. Past life therapy creates a sense of knowing and accepting your whole self as an immor-tal spiritual being on a human journey.

Lifescript

A lifescript is made up of all the 'oughts and shoulds', the 'I musts' and the conditioned responses and expectations arising from the past – whenever that past was. It is the sum total of all our karmic experience and it includes our lessons and inten-tions for the present life. If we follow a lifescript unconsciously, we rerun all the old patterns. Changing our lifescript can bring about profound healing at all levels of our life.

Past life therapy teaches us that the conditions we encounter in our present life are not simply a punishment for 'bad karma' – our misdeeds in a former life. Nevertheless, it may well pin-point where we are inflicting misery on ourselves as a way of 'shriving our guilt' from the past. It shows us that, as spiritual beings, we are part of a lives-long learning process. We may need to experience what we construe, from the limited perspective of our present earthly life, as an 'awful life' in order to balance out other experiences, or to round out our compassion and empathy for other people. It shows us the long, intricate strands of our relationships weaving their way through many roles and interactions over dozens of lifetimes. It can also teach us that the people we think hate us most, in fact love us enough to put us through hell. Not because we deserve it, or as a punishment, but because we have chosen to learn that particular lesson, to have that necessary experience.

The regression techniques used to reach the past life cause can include hypnosis, deep meditation, guided imagery, shamanic journeys, massage and bodywork. All entail a change of consciousness, a moving out of ordinary, everyday awareness. This enables 'time travel' to take place, a moving back in time to re-experience the incident. By reframing this incident, if necessary, healing takes place. For convenience, in order to make sense of our experiences, these other lives are called past lives, although time is by no means linear nor chronological. However, by 'going back into the past', we can change our present life.

Blockages

A point where we are stuck in the past. Blockages may be physical and bodily-based, emotional, mental or spiritual. An ingrained attitude such as 'poor me' (victim mentality) is a blockage as it impedes well-being. An old scar or wound, invisible though it may be in the present life, may block the free flow of energy through the body creating a state of disease or illness.

Our 'personal consciousness', or self awareness has several levels, or sub-strata, some of which incorporate 'universal consciousness' and connect us with everything around us – and all that has gone before.

Besides our everyday, ordinary awareness, we have a hidden consciousness of which we are only dimly aware. This is the subconscious, the repository of all our experiences, memories, dreams, hopes and expectations. The subconscious mind motivates much of our experience in life, without us being aware of it. We repeat patterns, live out ingrained expectations, follow its dictates. Much of the contents of our subconscious mind are the direct opposite of what we consciously think. By accessing the subconscious we can change our behaviour and heal our dis-ease.

Beneath the subconscious is the unconscious, the collective unconscious as Jung called it, where lurk family and racial memories going back into pre-history. This too has a powerful effect on our lives. The collective unconscious is global and universal, we share it with everyone else.

Surrounding all of this is the 'higher consciousness' of our spiritual self. Time does not exist for the higher consciousness. This consciousness is past, present and future – there is no distinction. Higher consciousness is more than global, it is cosmic: we are everything else at this level.

In past life work, all these levels of consciousness may be activated.

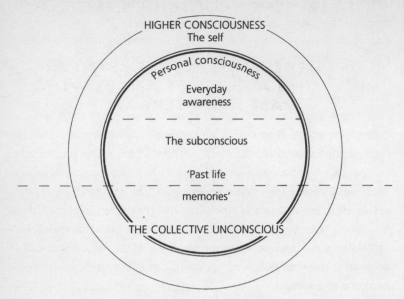

The Levels of Consciousness

IS RELIVING A LIFE ENOUGH?

It depends on your reason for regressing. It is sufficient to satisfy curiosity, to give a sense of: 'Yes, I have lived before'. It may give you an insight into what is going on. However, as Denys Kelsey, one of the pioneers of past life therapy, puts it: "Insight does not necessarily imply cure." Simply reliving a life is rarely enough for more serious purposes. Most of the therapeutic work involves freeing something which has become stuck in the past, the burden of which has been carried forward into the present. That burden may have created a pattern of reaction, based on the now inappropriate past. This pattern needs to be rewoven so that a new response is possible. The primary cause may be emotional, physical or mental, but it will imprint on the present life and may be experienced as some form of illness or other dis-ease, not necessarily physical. Past life therapy seeks to clear the cause, and the dis-ease is healed.

IS THERE A DIFFERENCE BETWEEN RELIVING A PAST LIFE AND HAVING PAST LIFE THERAPY?

Most definitely. Rerunning a past life is for the curious. The 'who was I' approach is not therapeutic. It rarely makes any major difference to your present life or brings about permanent change. It may give an insight, an 'Aha, so that's why ...' moment. It may also boost your ego for a short time, depending on the experience. But the effect usually fades.

The therapy approach uncovers the reasons behind your present behaviour or difficulty and changes the picture. It expands your understanding of yourself. Therapy means healing. It is curative. Your life or health should improve, sometimes dramatically, after past life therapy.

WILL I RETAIN CONTROL OF THE PROCESS?

It all depends on the method used and on the individual therapist. Some regression therapists are strongly directive, retaining control of the process at all times; others work with a client-centred approach that allows the client to work at their own pace and in their own way (with help or direction from the therapist when needed).

CAN OTHER PEOPLE 'SEE' MY PAST LIVES?

Yes. Psychics, astrologers and shamans all have ways of reading past lives for other people. I use a combination of astrology and far memory to do karmic readings, for example. When I first started doing this work I would see lives unrolling in front of my eyes just like watching a film. It was most graphic. If I looked at someone's face, I would see their past life faces superimposed. I still use this ability, but now 'see' much more subjectively, and often work without meeting my client face to face.

Far Memory

The psychic ability to tune into other lives,
whether one's own or other people's.

Some psychics and shamans use 'far memory', some contact your Higher Self, others contact a guide who knows your past, while others may use a 'set formula'. One astrological approach has a formula which purports to tell you exactly who you were, whilst karmic astrology identifies your patterns and probable experiences but not the precise detail of your lives. People reading for you may use the aura, the Akashic Record or the birthchart, or journey into other realms to gather information. These readings can be extremely useful in giving you an overview, or in pinpointing particular problems. Sometimes simply knowing, accepting at a deep inner level: "This is true for me," is enough to recognize the root cause or change the pattern. At other times this is a starting point for personal regression work. Indeed, some regressionists work by tuning into a past life for you and having you tune in too.

Guides

Guides are discarnate beings, that is they inhabit the spiritual dimensions rather than the physical. They come to assist us when required. It is widely believed that our guides are souls who have known us in other lives, although it is also possible that they are another aspect of ourself.

There are psychics who can enter into the other life with you, using their energy to bring about change. They are fully involved with you as you were then, feeling what you felt (or feel, if you yourself are doing the regression). At a subtle level they heal the past and you receive the benefit in your present life. Joan Grant and Christine Hartley frequently utilized this approach. I may do so myself during karmic readings or regression sessions but I prefer to facilitate my clients doing the work themselves in regression as I believe we each need to take responsibility for our own healing. Shamans, particularly those using North or South American Indian methods, may well journey to your past lives, 'recovering' a lost part of yourself, bringing it back and helping you to integrate this into your present life.

The Akashic Record

The Akashic Record is an esoteric narrative of all that has been, and will be. It is woven into the fabric of the universe. It encompasses all possibilities. It can be 'read' by psychics, amongst others, to give details of past lives and present purpose.

The Higher Self

The eternal, spiritual part of us that is immortal and which, because it experiences all our lives, contains our totality of being. It is 'higher' because it is vibrating at a faster rate than the physical body.

THE ADVANTAGES AND THE DANGERS

The advantage of any form of past life therapy is that it enables extremely deep change to take place at the source of the problem. It is not dealing with symptoms, it addresses the cause. In fully experiencing or reliving the past, in reconnecting to lost parts of the self, in integrating previously unacceptable facets or in allowing oneself to fully feel the feelings and emotions of that life, and in reframing and rewriting the past, profound healing takes place.

The greatest danger lies perhaps in the ego. If there is an underlying need to compensate for any feelings of inadequacy in the present life, then an ego trip is an ever-present possibility. So too is getting caught up in a 'fantasy in fancy dress'; wishful thinking is hardly therapeutic. An experienced practitioner will know how to recognize a fantasy, and how to work with it symbolically to bring about healing. The danger from the practitioner's ego arises when the practitioner is over-confident: "I've seen it all, I can handle everything." Life has a funny way of throwing up a few surprises, so retaining humility and the ability to learn on the job are vital.

The other great danger lies in practitioners who are inexperienced and/or unable or unwilling to stay with the process if deep trauma surfaces. Many hypnotists immediately instruct their clients to forget all about it, thus driving the trauma even deeper. Other practitioners tell their clients to detach, to move away from the experience instead of reliving the pain and blocked emotions that they failed to allow themselves to feel the first time round: thus perpetuating the blockage. They try to 'make it better', putting a plaster on it rather than real healing – which may require cauterization and catharsis. Just because it is forgotten at the conscious level does not mean it goes away. It wreaks havoc from the depths of the unconscious. The opposite may apply, someone may go back into an emotion in which they are endlessly stuck, recreating the situation from which they need to detach. Different problems require different solutions and the therapist must be flexible enough to deal with whatever comes up. The danger is that, if, for instance, someone relives having their leg blown off and the trauma is not healed once they are the other side of death, then leg problems may well be triggered in the present life as the 'seed' is activated.

A subtle danger may arise from reactivating a past life 'tendency' or life state not relevant to the present life (or which it was hoped to reverse) but which is brought into the present through not being released when the regression finishes. For example, a man reconnected to several lives where he had been celibate and deeply spiritual. In his present life he was married and following a spiritual pathway. After the past lives surfaced, he suddenly felt that he could no longer follow his spiritual path and remain married. He turned away from his wife, excluding her from his life and accusing her of sabotaging his spirituality. His astrological chart indicated that his purpose in incarnating this time round had been to learn to be both spiritual and sexual at the same time – something he had been unable to do in the past. He had the opportunity to heal a deep split in himself. It would have been relevant, following the many celibate lives he relived, to ask whether the vows of celibacy by which he was then bound were appropriate for his present life.

Had the answer been 'no', then steps could have been taken to release himself from that vow. As it was, not only was his marriage destroyed, but he cut himself off from the potential to heal the two warring factions within himself.

A similar danger arises where people are told, or choose to believe, they are soulmates, that they have always been together and should be together again. I have seen marriages wrecked, relationships ruined, people devastated. Suddenly recognizing someone as a past soulmate can cause a wave of lust to arise that carries all before it, and may well obscure the real purpose in meeting again. Disentangling is difficult. So it is as well to look exceedingly closely at any potential 'soulmate' relationship and to check whether that really was what you intended this time around.

Soulmates

Sometimes called twin flames or twin souls, soulmates are often seen as two people (or souls) who have been together throughout eternity. They are 'meant for each other', complete each other. Plato said that, way back in the beginning, one soul had split into two, creating soulmates. (He also said that 'ever the two shall wander, seeking each other').

However, from regression work it would appear that we all have several soulmates, a group of souls with whom we travel throughout time. It is also apparent that our soulmate is often the person who is willing to help us learn the hardest lessons in life.

THOSE FOR WHOM IT MAY BE UNSUITABLE

Whilst it is possible that past life therapy may help a schizophrenic or Multiple Personality Disorder sufferer to bring together parts of a psyche that are fragmented, it needs an extremely experienced therapist to undertake this work. As a rule of thumb, anyone who has had psychiatric problems of any kind or who is taking drugs (prescription or otherwise) should approach the therapy with caution and should certainly be totally honest with any prospective therapist. Past life therapy can help, sometimes dramatically, with depression, phobias and some compulsive patterns. But it can also precipitate compulsions and obsessions of all kinds and may bolster up delusions and illusions through an apparent 'reliving'. People with psychiatric problems could, therefore, find the overview offered by a past life reading, or karmic astrology, a gentler introduction to other lives.

People who are prone to fantasy, and to living in the past, can use other lives as an excuse for not living the present life fully. Equally, it is possible to become obsessed by a character in a past life, or to become stuck in an old pattern. So many people say, "I can't help it, it's my karma," notwithstanding the fact that past life therapy is designed to prove just the opposite. So, if you fall into these categories or are not yet ready to take responsibility for your own life (or lives), you may find a bodywork, emotional release or shamanic-based approach keeps you more grounded in the here and now whilst releasing from the past life patterns.

Anyone out to prove they were 'Someone' may have difficulty with past life therapy. They may well reject perfectly valid lives, and the healing opportunities they embody, in the search for that elusive 'proof' of position, power and authority. This

approach is extremely vulnerable to fantasy and wish fulfilment, both on the part of the practitioner and the client. Hypnosis is probably the best approach if you must have facts, figures and historical presence.

Finally, anyone not prepared to look at their dark side should certainly steer clear of this therapy. It throws light on all of ourselves, not just those parts we find pleasing. Its value is that it helps to integrate our totality. But, if you are not ready for what this might entail, you are not yet ready to look at your past lives.

USING PAST LIFE WORK IN CONJUNCTION WITH OTHER THERAPIES

Past life work deepens and expands psychotherapy, bodywork, emotional release and spiritual growth work. It combines well with flower essences and vibrational medicine, reflexology, crystal healing and many other complementary therapies.

POSSIBLE
PAST LIFE CAUSES

E ach individual case is different, but 'themes' or common core experiences often underlie similar presenting problems. A few of these are explored below to give you an idea of the scope of past life therapy.

PHOBIAS

Many people consult past life therapists about phobias or chronic anxiety states of one kind or another. If the cause has not been found in a previous incident in the present life, then even conventional therapy might suggest exploring other lives. A common phobia such as fear of snakes, for instance, may well go back to a death from snake bite, or being lowered into a pit of snakes (sometimes as punishment, sometimes as an initiation). I have seen a case where fear of birds went back to being very badly injured in a battle, and regaining consciousness to find a flock of vultures pecking away at the apparently dead body.

A phobia which is seemingly much less common, but which I have frequently encountered, is fear of people vomiting. Almost everyone who suffers from this has regressed to a life where they were with a group of other people, usually in conditions of fear, who were vomiting uncontrollably. In at least one case it was on a ship during a violent storm, in several others it was during some kind of plague when all the sufferers were locked in a room together. It may also relate to one's own death under such conditions.

Sometimes phobias are very specific. I had one client, for example, who could not stand deep, still water. She was fine with running water, rivers and seas. In the regression, she had drowned in a quarry pool.

Once the past life cause is discovered and healing done at that point in time, the phobia usually disappears or significantly decreases in the present life.

EATING DISORDERS

Whilst many eating disorders do have roots in emotional causes in early childhood, some may be a carry-over from other lives. A common cause of over-eating is starving to death in the past, especially when the last thought in that life was, "I'll never starve again," but I have also seen the then socially-acceptable practice of bulimic vomiting at Roman orgies being carried over into the present life as a repeating pattern. (This also surfaced in a fear of vomiting when the slave who looked after the vomitorium was run through with a dagger for himself involuntarily vomiting as his master did so.)

Anorexia too may be linked to past life beliefs about the body as 'bad' and sexuality as sinful and can link into past life sexual abuse. Fashion can play its part. Not that long ago, many girls starved themselves in England, for instance, in order to achieve the desired eighteen-inch waist.

If patterns like these are not changed prior to the new incarnation, the hidden thoughts remain and create over-eating, bulimia and anorexia. Going back to the between life state can be therapeutic.

There are so many emotional blockages carried over that it is unusual not to encounter one or two during a regression session. Emotional blockages often surface spontaneously during bodywork as our physical body can hold the memory. The blockages arise from two basic causes: one, part of oneself being stuck in that old emotion, continually re-experiencing it; or, two, having been afraid to feel the feelings, continually holding back. The trauma may be too intense, we cannot allow ourselves to feel. But so many of our emotions are deemed unacceptable that we get into the habit of not feeling. The healing consists of either detaching from the feeling, or letting oneself feel it until it dissipates – acceptance is a great healer.

ADDICTIONS

If we die with the thought "There will never be enough …", or desiring "More, more," then we are likely to come back with an addictive personality. If the thought was, "There will never be enough love," then the addiction is to relationships and what passes for 'love'. If it was 'money', then the addiction is to material goods – the miser hoarding his wealth. On the other hand, that person may still be stuck in poverty consciousness: believing that there will never be enough money is often enough to ensure that there never is!

Denys Kelsey mentions addiction being linked to the practice of giving alcohol to deaden the pain of surgery in the days before anaesthetics. In battle conditions, on ships, etc, a bottle would be passed around those awaiting the surgeon's knife. At least one alcoholic he regressed died with the thought: "There won't be enough for me."

People with this kind of strong desire often reincarnate quickly before any healing has been done, bringing the potential for the dependency back into the body. Something which has always struck me in my alcohol and drug counselling work is how young people are when they discover their 'drug of choice'. I remember an alcoholic telling me with great relish that, aged 8, he drank a whole bottle of sherry and felt for the first time that he was totally satisfied: "It was something I had been looking for all my young life."

Some drug addictions continually re-run an earlier dependency on 'medicine': sleeping drops, 'nerve tonics', etc, which contained morphine or other addictive substances. Laudanum was very popular with several generations of women. In some cultures, drugs were routinely used either as sedatives or as spiritual aids. Other addicts may be replaying an opium addiction – thousands of Chinese were introduced to opium by the British government who had a vested interest in maintaining the addiction; and the gin palaces of the British Industrial Revolution killed the pain of existence for many thousands more people.

HEALTH

Health is an enormous subject when looked at from the past life perspective. Old attitudes such as 'hard-heartedness' can affect the present life: hardening of the arteries and heart attacks being common manifestations. Old emotions, injuries and traumatic experiences create physical dis-ease. A woman who had constant heartburn in her present life relived drinking a cup of poisoned wine given her by a lover. The heartburn was easily cured by erasing the memory of the poison through her imaging drinking the antidote. We can also recreate our old feelings when we put ourselves in present life situations which resonate.

Before therapy, having her current-life lover feed her a tempting morsel had almost choked her, as she could never be quite sure that he wasn't trying to kill her.

The past life reasons behind present life illness are sometimes dramatic. An elderly lady had suffered from asthma all her life. When she arrived for regression she brought with her not only an inhaler but also a friend who was skilled in resuscitation techniques and had revived her on more than one occasion. In the event, however, neither were needed.

She was guided back through time until she found herself in the Middle Ages acting as a kind of go-between who received the reports from spies and informers and passed these on to the witch-finders. It was something in which she had unwittingly become embroiled and could not then break free. She described herself as an insignificant looking, lonely man. He felt suffocated by what he was doing but could see no way out. If he tried to leave or to protect people, he would be put to trial by his employers as they would assume that he had been bewitched. He wanted to commit suicide but this was a mortal sin and he was too afraid of the consequences.

Eventually the burden became too great to bear and he took a horse and rode off without caring what would happen. He was followed and was stabbed by a sword, which caused him to fall from the horse. The horse then rolled on him, crushing his chest. He died literally unable to breathe and gasped his life away in a most distressing manner that exactly matched an asthma attack. As the elderly lady relived it, the physical symptoms were very real. She gasped and fought for breath, making the most horrendous noises. But, because she was both reliving that life and aware of the present connections, she would assure me from time to time that she was ok. This was not an asthma attack. Knowing that she needed to go through this, I encouraged her to stay with it as she passed through death and into

20   the between life state. There, the trauma fell away. Her breathing quieted, almost to the point of imperceptibility. We cleared
the residues of that life to heal the present.

When she 'returned' from the regression, she was full of compassion for herself as she had been, saying that he had had no
choice. What surprised her was how afraid to commit suicide
he had been as, in her present life, that would have been what
she would have done in a similar situation. It is difficult to
believe nowadays just how great the fear of mortal sin and
resulting everlasting damnation was but this had graphically
portrayed itself to her. The fear had been even stronger than the
feelings of guilt and wrongness, which were in themselves
overwhelming. With that kind of inner conflict combined with
violent death, it was no surprise that her current life played out
the drama in such a physical fashion.

She recognized that her asthma was the direct result of both
the sense of suffocation and guilt that she had felt then, and
also the physical sensation of her death. It had imprinted itself
on her present-life body, which continued to 'gasp her life
away'. It also explained why she had become a pioneering psychic and healer. She wanted to make reparation. Her compassion and forgiveness for herself healed the root cause.
Following the regression, her asthma attacks ceased.

Several points of 'dis-ease' may arise from one life. Muriel
relived a life in the theatre. She was badly beaten by the manager of that theatre, who was jealous of her success. He constantly
criticized her: "She was no good" (despite the fact that she was
a very good actress). She could not break free and felt most
inadequate. Much of the beating was on her back. In her present life, Muriel suffered from constant sore throats, back trouble and lack of confidence. These conditions were exacerbated
when she and her partner got involved in amateur dramatics.
She felt that her partner was that theatre manager.

In the regression, she went to the end of her life. She hung herself on the stage, in a most dramatic fashion, saying, "That will show them all." She wanted to be seen when 'they' entered the theatre the next day. She wanted 'them' to be affected by her death. She wanted 'them' to notice her. The death was a slow one, her neck not being broken, and she suffocated to death. Muriel commented that it explained why, in her present life, she could never complete a performance without having a sore throat and a cold. She associated the slow asphyxiation and pressure of the rope around her neck with the current life throat trouble but also felt that she was in some way sabotaging herself as a result of that constant criticism in the past.

However, the 'dis-ease' went deeper than that. As a teenager, Muriel had suffered from nocturnal epilepsy. A chiropracter had then realigned the vertebrae in her neck, and she never suffered another fit. In the regression, she commented that her body jerking at the end of the rope was just like having convulsions. As her neck was not broken, the vertebrae were pushed out of alignment. In her present life, her 'etheric blueprint' had recreated that pattern.

When we began to look at the healing options, she simply wanted to leave that body there. To get away as quickly as possible and go into the halls of healing, which she described as 'absolute bliss'. In a spontaneous soul retrieval, she then saw a man rushing in and taking her in a 1950s taxi to the hospital where she was born.

It became clear that, whilst that part of herself had 'slept' in the halls of healing, other parts of Muriel had had other lives. In order to be born whole in this present life, that 'sleeping part' had had to be rushed to join the rest of herself at birth. Its memories had been activated when she went back into the theatre. Past life therapy then healed the 'cause' and she was able to perform without difficulties. Later, when she visited a

chiropracter again, she saw herself just prior to putting the rope around her neck. Her guide said to her, "You don't have to damage your body, you have come to the end of that life and can come with me." She then saw the empty rope. The situation had been reframed and her body was able to release the memory.

> ### Soul retrieval
>
> Reconnecting to a part of the overall self that has been 'left behind' in a past life.

> ### Etheric Blueprint
>
> The 'seed' from which the physical body develops in the present life. The etheric blueprint carries all the information, and scars, from past lives that will affect emotional and physical health and well-being in the life to come.

SEXUAL DIFFICULTIES

Sexual difficulties too can stem from varied past life causes. One of the most common problems is that vows, such as celibacy or everlasting faithfulness, taken in other lives are not rescinded before reincarnation. They then subtly interfere with present life relationships. Having taken a vow of celibacy, for example, may result in impotence when faced with a sexual partner. The subconscious can simply switch off sexual arousal when confronted with the deep inner conflict of 'I desire this woman' and 'I vow eternal celibacy'. The time frame may need to be renegotiated: 'for ever' becoming 'for this life only'.

Old patterns of behaviour can also be carried over. Some people endlessly recreate their past relationships, sometimes compelled by a vision of what they did not have, at others obsessed with the search for what they did have. They may also carry inappropriate patterns of behaviour. One man, suffering from premature ejaculation, experienced furtive sex with another servant in his past life. There was always an urgent need to 'be quick', someone might find them. Another man was sexually hung up on his mother. All his fantasies were about sex with her. Not surprisingly, he regressed to being her lover in a former life.

More difficult to adjust to are gender changes which can create underlying problems. Both men and women find themselves 'in the wrong body'. Some necessitate a sex change, others respond to past life therapy. Some conditions are complex. Not every case of homosexuality necessarily relates to a man having been a woman before and retaining the desire for sexual contact with a man (or vice versa), but some do. If that person is happy to accept their sexual orientation, then all is well. But it can create a painful conflict in someone who cannot adapt or who comes under pressure to conform to 'a norm'. (Most homosexuals and lesbians are following their consciously-made life plan just as heterosexuals are, their orientation is different not wrong.)

I regressed a woman who said she had always felt like a young boy with homosexual tendencies. She 'fancied older men'. This did not appear on the surface as a problem because older men were only too pleased to have an affair with this attractive woman. But, inside herself she felt cheated. She was in the wrong body for the experience she craved. When she regressed, she was indeed a young homosexual. In the between life state, she had wanted to experience life in a woman's body but she had not sufficiently planned and programmed her new identity. The old patterns took over.

REGRESSION TECHNIQUES

The techniques used to induce regression are many and varied. Some have been in existence for immeasurable time, others are new. Shamans, and other spiritual disciplines, have used drugs, chanting and repetitive dance to induce trance states for hundreds of years. In a trance state there are no boundaries, time does not exist. Memories can be accessed, knowledge harvested, blockages removed. The shamanic culture is both ancient and universal. The note of a Buddhist cymbal, or an African tribal drum, will take you into a different state of being. Sound, smell and touch can stimulate memory, as can places or people.

Some therapists will use touch, others imagery, some hypnosis, but all are creating an altered state of consciousness in which it is possible to access the otherwise inaccessible parts of our being. Many start by achieving a state of deep relaxation, others by pressing appropriate parts of the body. Regression may be incidental to the main purpose of the technique as in body or energy based therapies such as Shen, Shiatsu, Process Acupressure, etc, where the intention is to release an energy blockage rather than necessarily stimulate past life memories. Many regression therapists combine several different approaches in their therapeutic work.

HYPNOTIC TRANCE

An artificially induced state of so-called 'sleep', deep relaxation or altered awareness, is called 'trance'. From brainwave measurements, it is clearly not sleep as the brain remains active. The subject may, when brought out of trance, be unaware of actions or activities undertaken in this state, although in many levels of hypnosis the subject is fully aware of what is going on and retains that consciousness. Hypnosis accesses the subconscious mind, that level of consciousness that lies 'beneath' ordinary, everyday awareness, and which retains all our memories. The subconscious mind is extremely powerful and can bring about deep healing.

There is a difference between a hypnotist, who merely accesses the memories, and a hypnotherapist, who uses those memories therapeutically to effect change.

In hypnotic trance, the subject is directed back through time or told to go straight to a particular time or experience. Appropriate questions are used to guide the process. Control of the experience remains with the therapist.

Regression under hypnosis is vivid, the subject experiences all the feelings, pains and joys of the life. The therapeutic value varies according to whether or not the therapist believes rerunning the life is all that is required and whether the therapist recognizes symbolic and other states. If healing and reframing techniques are also used, the therapeutic value of the experience is likely to be enhanced and longer lasting.

ACTIVE IMAGINATION

In active imagination, the subject is encouraged to 'act as if' until the scene becomes real. So, for instance, the therapist may 'see' the scene first, describing it until the subject joins in; or may direct the subject through various actions such as opening a wardrobe and selecting clothing. Control of the process is transferred to the subject when possible.

The reliving of a life may be graphic or gentle. As with hypnosis, the long-term benefit depends on the approach employed by the therapist. One of the advantages of this technique is that the subject can experience the life at different depths according to what is necessary for healing to take place. This technique is an excellent introduction to past life work and can be a powerful therapeutic tool according to the level of expertise of the therapist and the ancillary techniques employed.

GUIDED IMAGERY

Guided imagery may be rather like active imagination. After entering a state of deep relaxation, the subject is taken on a journey which will lead into a past life image. Appropriate questions such as: "What are you wearing," "How do you feel," may be used to guide the experience. Control of the process remains with the subject, facilitated where necessary by the therapist.

The reliving of a life may be graphic or gentle. As with hypnosis and active imagination, the long-term benefit depends on the approach employed by the therapist. The subject can experience the life at different depths as required. An excellent introduction to past life work, it can be a powerful therapeutic tool.

In the Christos technique, deep relaxation is induced by rubbing the feet and the forehead, a process which can take some time. Guided imagery is then used to direct the subject to another life, although the subject may spontaneously flip into another life. Control of the process generally remains with the subject.

The disadvantage of this technique is the length of time that may be required to induce the change in consciousness. It is, however, a useful tool for experiencing a past life. Reliving can be graphic, but it may prove difficult to change levels in order for healing work to take place. As with all the approaches, the individual therapist will profoundly affect the therapeutic value of the work.

SHAMANIC JOURNEYS

Shamanic journeys may be undertaken by the shaman on behalf of the subject, or by the subject guided by the shaman. In native cultures, drugs are often used to facilitate the change of consciousness needed. Sound, drums or chanting, along with rhythmic movement may also be used. Control of the process generally remains with the shaman (much less so in drug-induced trance) although guidance may be limited.

In cases where the shaman makes the journey, the therapeutic value is often profound. When the subject makes the journey, much will depend on how able they are to stay with the process and how much therapeutic input the shaman has.

SOUL RETRIEVAL

A similar process to a shamanic journey or guided imagery, although hypnosis may be used as a way into the experience. In soul retrieval, a 'piece of the soul' is seen as being stuck in other lives or childhood experiences. The subject or the shaman will journey to the place where that piece of soul is held in order to free it and reintegrate it in the present life. Control of the process depends on the technique used and the individual practitioner.

As with shamanic journeys, in cases where the shaman makes the journey, the therapeutic value is often profound. When the subject makes the journey, much will depend on how able they are to stay with the process and how much therapeutic input the shaman has.

PAST LIFE HEALING

Past life healing combines elements of regression, guided journeys, soul retrieval and emotional release. It is direct experience of the other life or lives in order to clear blockages. It can also encompass the between life state and birth into the present life in order to be fully present.

The process is facilitated by the therapist but control remains with the client.

BODYWORK

As the name suggests, bodywork is practised directly on the physical body. Approaches vary from massage and manipulation to acting out expression of feelings, scenarios, etc. Many types of bodywork, intentionally or inadvertently, trigger past life memories. In most, the memory arises out of movement, massage or pressure on a particular point. This may be a known trigger point, the site of an energy block or old wound, or the part of the body that holds the memory. Kinesiology, or muscle testing, can quickly identify if a past life is responsible for a present life symptom and can remove the imprint from the present life body.

In some types of bodywork, active and vigorous physical expression is used to work through the issues raised by the memory. So, for instance, if someone is reliving being held down, they will be actively encouraged to physically fight off the person restraining them: the therapist, playing the part of the aggressor, using cushions, mattresses, etc as needed. In other types of bodywork, once the memory has been activated, it will proceed through active imagination or imagery depending on the therapist's inclination and training.

The effect of bodywork can be very powerful indeed. It is particularly useful where past life causes have manifested as illness or emotional blocks in the present life. The past life memory often surfaces graphically. Much will depend on the level of therapeutic intervention by the therapist, and how much the work is an uncontrolled, undirected catharsis or release of energy.

FAR MEMORY

When far memory is used for therapy, the practitioner will tune into relevant past lives, passing on the insights gained to the client. The practitioner may also use healing energy to enter into the other life and so bring about change which carries forward into the present. The client may or may not enter into that past life themselves. The value depends on how accurately the practitioner can tune into other lives and how the information is utilized. It is essential that the practitioner is

capable of guiding a past life therapeutically should the client spontaneously regress.

This technique is helpful in gaining an overview of lives, for identifying patterns and connections and for suggesting a psychotherapeutic approach in the present life. If the practitioner has powerful healing skills and knows how to direct these properly, deep healing can take place at a soul level. Far memory may trigger a profound recognition and knowing in the client, precipitating them into reliving the life or into a spontaneous catharsis or change of pattern.

WHAT TO EXPECT

As both the way into a past life and its content vary so widely, there is no such thing as a 'typical session'. I have, however, included examples from different approaches at the end of this chapter.

At the first session most therapists will want to know something of your background and your reasons for seeking therapy. Some will devote a preliminary session to this, usually around 40 to 50 minutes. They are looking for the key phrases and themes that will provide a way in. Others will take this 'history' as part of the settling down process, helping you to feel comfortable before the actual regression begins. In this case, you will probably find the session is about 1½ to 2 hours in duration, although some people will fit it into the 'therapeutic hour' (55 minutes) and other techniques can take much longer.

Induction procedures, actually getting you into the past life, vary in length from a few moments to perhaps up to half an hour or longer. This will naturally affect the length of the session. If the session is part of an on-going process, then the therapist may check what has been happening to you since you last met before beginning the new regression. Some therapists like to take time at the end to discuss what happened and to integrate the work. Others do this as the session proceeds.

For the actual regression, depending on how he or she works, the therapist may ask you to sit in a chair, or lie on a bed, massage couch or the floor. You will be fully clothed, unless the approach entails massage of any kind. Many therapists wrap their client in a blanket as the body can get extremely cold during regression (this is due to energy changes, not the temperature of the room). Music may be playing, joss sticks might scent the air. Almost all techniques start with some kind of relaxation, time for you to leave the outside world behind and bring your attention into yourself. Most therapists like to have a few moments to attune to your energies.

We will see later in this chapter how the session might proceed from here.

NUMBER OF SESSIONS

The number of sessions depends on the practitioner's approach and what you are seeking. A phobia may disappear after only one session, or may take several regressions to uncover the core life. A deeply traumatic life may surface explosively at the first session, or need gradual exposure over many weeks. Frequency also varies according to the practitioner. If the therapy is part of an intense, on-going therapy or bodywork process, sessions may take place once or even twice weekly. Other approaches need integration time in between sessions, so monthly or even longer intervals may be appropriate.

WILL I REMEMBER?

Almost certainly, unless you are working with a hypnotherapist who commands you to forget. Most people retain a vivid memory of the past life, or lives, they have experienced during a session (years later they remember it as though it were yesterday).

Some practitioners tape the session, others make notes. Keeping your own record after a session is useful as it helps the pieces to fall into place. However, if the session covered events or experiences that you needed to release from, it can be counterproductive to go over them again afterwards.

WILL I BE THE SAME SEX AS I AM NOW?

Maybe. The overwhelming evidence from regressions is that we experience lives as both male and female. So don't be surprised if you do change sex. However, there are therapists who believe we retain the same sex all the time. If you are being regressed by one of these therapists, then you may be influenced by what the therapist believes is possible – and, of course, by what you believe. The actual words the therapist uses, consciously or unconsciously, especially those pertaining to gender, can greatly affect what you experience.

WILL I RECOGNISE ANYONE?

Quite likely. We do tend to be with the same people in other lives, especially our families but also people who are now on the periphery of our life. It is doubtful that they will look exactly the same as they do now although this has been known, they may even be a different sex. They may take completely different roles. But people do suddenly say: "Oh, it's so and so. There is something about the eyes." (It is said the eyes are the window to the soul and these are what people recognize most frequently.)

A client of mine says that, in this present life, she saw the back of her husband's neck when he was walking down the street and recognized it from a past life. "I just knew I had to marry him." She finally met him a few years later, and again 'recognized' him from the back. When we explored their old

connections, in one life he was a gaoler who was particularly kind to her. He spent a great deal of time stationed outside her cell. All she saw of him was the back of his neck through the peephole in the door.

Be prepared for some surprises. Just because we are married to someone now does not mean that person cannot be our mother or father, child, next-door neighbour, most hated enemy, etc, in another life.

WILL I ALWAYS BE HUMAN?

Well here again it does seem to depend on your own and the practitioner's beliefs as to whether you touch a life where you have non-human form. The Sufi poet Rumi said:

I died as a mineral and became a plant
I died as a plant and rose to animal
I died as animal and I was Man.
Why should I fear? When was I less by dying?
Yet once more I shall die as Man, to soar
With Angels blest, but even from angelhood
I must pass on.

There is one English therapist who always takes people back to when they were animals, plants, crystals. He was most surprised when I said people rarely experienced this with me, although I have known it to happen. One woman had a profound experience of spiritual being: in the form of an amethyst crystal. I recognize that consciousness can take many forms, but I suspect that many experiences of going into animal form could well have something to do with the shamanic practices of our ancestors, or could be a symbolic analogy.

'Life' does not always have to happen on earth. Many people

report 'alien life form' lives, sometimes on earth but more usually elsewhere in the universe. I once took someone back to find out about his fear of flying, and was somewhat surprised (as he was) to find him crash landing a space ship and living a very lonely life unable to go 'home'. Home seemed to be a planet in the outer reaches of another star system. Before the regression, he had not considered the possibility of life in space.

You may also find yourself exploring the between life state. If you go to a high enough 'vibration', you may lose the sense of being an individual human being. Anything is possible.

HOW WILL I FEEL AFTER THE REGRESSION?

This depends on what happens. Feelings can vary from the highest elation to the deepest depression as experiences work their way out.

Initially, you may return to present life awareness feeling cold and a bit shivery. You may be exhausted or highly energized. You may feel totally with it, or somewhat spaced out. Many therapists give their clients a cup of tea at this stage, and some will use the subtle healing powers of flower essences or crystals to integrate the work that has been done. By the time you leave, however, you should be feeling much more normal. If the therapist is urging you to leave and you still feel ungrounded or spaced out, be sure to say so.

You may notice a difference in how you feel or respond to things immediately. Over the next few days, as you integrate the work, your attitude to life should improve; your sense of well-being increase. If you had a phobia, you should be much less anxious than you were. Indeed, you may feel able to confront the very thing that would have sent you running away in terror before. However, if previously locked-in emotions have

been released, you may need to allow these feelings to be there until they dissipate naturally or until you return to therapy. Be kind to yourself, take it easy, and don't expect too much too soon. On the other hand, you may go home feeling wonderful, euphoric. If so, don't be surprised if you come back to earth with a bang at some stage.

Moving around, doing something practical should soon get you settled into your everyday life again.

LEVELS OF REGRESSION

There are different levels, or depths, of regression, all of which may be experienced during past life therapy as each is relevant to a particular type of healing.

Some people vividly relive the past life experience. This is the deepest level. They are totally involved, feeling again exactly the emotions, and possibly the pain, that they felt at the time. They experience all the sensations. They smell the odours, hear the noises, feel the clothes they are wearing, the temperature of the air, the textures and moods of that life. They know the joys and sorrows intimately. They say: "This is my experience."

Others 'see' the life projected as though onto a screen, an experience from which they are somewhat detached and with which they have little physical or emotional involvement. It could be happening to someone else, it may be imagination. They ask: "Is this real? Is it mine?." At this level, the person may be looking down on the scene, not quite knowing who they are or what is happening. They may feel like they are making it up, as though it is a fantasy. Or they may express it as: "He is just looking on, waiting." At this level, they need prompting to act.

Some people 'feel' the experience, they may never actually 'see' anything. Their body is tight, tense, anxious, wounded maybe. They may have a sense of oppression, of loss, cold, hunger, fear or rage. These feelings are real, the emotions sometimes overwhelming and, if they have been cut off for a long time, they are unfamiliar and somewhat puzzling. The person says, "These feelings are so strong," but may wonder, "Can they be mine?" depending on the level reached and the depth of involvement.

Glimpses of lives are common in the initial stages of regression, rather like tuning in a television set. Sometimes this links lives with a common thread but the detail need not be recovered. Much of it is snowflaky, blurred, it is difficult to catch but then, if appropriate, a picture comes into focus. It deepens, settles. The person moves into it. It becomes real.

Levels of regression

Level 1: 'Tuning in the television'. Blurred, occasional glimpses.

Level 2: 'Watching the movie'. Observing, non-participating.

Level 3: 'Acting the movie'. Sounds and some feelings but somewhat disconnected.

Level 4: 'Living it'. Involved but aware of present life also.

Level 5: 'I am'. Totally involved, unaware of anything else.

During the course of a regression, it is possible to move between the different levels several times. Indeed, this may be necessary if therapeutic work is to be done. You may need to feel the feelings, but being too immersed can show where you are stuck in the past.

Not all 'remembered' past lives are actually, factually true, as we shall see. But they are true for the person experiencing them: they are, in essence, part of that person's story and, as such, are therapeutically valuable. They have a psychological reality and validity. Such 'lives' may be symbolic, mythological, shared individual experience or a tapping into the universal, collective experience of humanity as a whole. This is, however, yet another level of regression.

Symbolic Regression

In a symbolic regression the person may appear to be reliving another life, but it is more an analogy to the present life than a past life experience. For instance, a woman who found herself searching an old house, eventually finding a safe in the attic in which an ancient key lay, was actually searching for knowledge inside herself. She was dissatisfied with her present life, particularly the career path she was on, but did not know how to move on. Following the 'regression', she studied astrology and shiatsu, both of which came naturally to her. The key unlocked buried talents and her life changed for the better. Strangely enough, her new career was in housing.

As not all regression is to other lives on earth, you may find yourself travelling into the post-death or pre-conception state of being: the between life state. This is the place where we assimilate and heal our past experiences. We also plan for future growth, so it is a useful space to enter as we can reconnect to the reasons for the present incarnation.

An experienced and flexible therapist will know exactly where his or her client is and what the therapeutic options are for healing and reconnection in that space. They will not try to force their own perspective on their client nor expect them to conform to a 'norm'.

In the example sessions below, the induction, or way in, is not included. Neither is the way out.

THE SHAMANIC APPROACH

I have chosen to begin with Tim's story, although in some ways it is a far from typical session because of its setting: a temple deep in the Peruvian jungle. However, many people are now making these shamanic journeys, whether with a native shaman in his natural setting or in the comfort of a practitioner's therapy room. Tim's experience is typical of the shamanic approach, although not all shamans will use a drug to bring the journey into being. Many use sound: chanting and drumming. Some burn herbs and other substances. Although it appeared to be haphazard, produced by the cactus, Tim's experience was carefully directed, at another level of consciousness, by the shaman. A shaman will stay with you, be aware of what you are going through as you journey.

Tim, aged 27, was one of a group of people who went to Peru on a month-long journey around ancient sites to meet native shamans. They followed the ancient shamanic practices, including the taking of the traditional plants. The journey was not an easy one in any sense, and it affected them all profoundly. Tim told me his story so that I could share it in this book.

On his shamanic journey he explored many facets of himself. Under the influence of one drug he felt like he was shattered, taken apart and then had to put himself back together again – a classic shamanic experience. Quite late on in the journey he had an experience which finally healed his birth, which had been induced. This experience shows how a past life can heal a present life difficulty by reconnecting to a time when it was different, when things went well.

"I was at a place called La Hoc, the temple of the Moon, in Peru with a local shaman, Augustine. We all sat outside in a circle and drank the San Pedro cactus. We went in one at a time, shutting our eyes.

"I knew it was going into the womb, you've got the vagina entrance and then the cave which was the womb. You follow the passage in, feeling the snake, feeling the energy – it's like living rock. I lay in a foetal position with my head over this circular hole that felt very, very deep, it went on forever. I felt secure, good. I shut my eyes and let go.

"I started to connect with my birth into this present life. It wasn't a conscious decision, it just happened and I went with it. I was aware of being with a twin, and then experiencing the miscarriage [of his twin] and the pain of that. It was really heart wrenching. It was like losing someone, a relationship breaking up.

"I connected with the fact that whenever a relationship was breaking up I would go right down into the worst pain of loss, and that the loss was coming from losing my twin.

"I was shown that birth sets you up for your whole life. The energy that you are born into is important and very special. Whatever that energy is, you're implanted with that dynamic. Like your birth chart: that is your energy.

"I felt also the pain of losing the other half, of how I have carried that pain all my life, in everyday life it has always been there. It affects how I do things. I also felt how I did not want to be born because of that loss. I wanted to stay in the womb because it was a safe space and nearer to where I had come from.

"Then the healing of the birth started. By being shown everything, it was transmuted at the same time."

People in the cave began drumming and past life recall occurred:

"It was like the sound came from outside the cave and came through, triggering the memory. It was a slow drumming to start with and it made me aware that it was a birth drum.

"I went into a teepee, in a womb as a baby, a native American. It wasn't just a teepee, it was a birth teepee, a sacred space. The mother was in the teepee and there were other women there too and they had prepared a space for the birth. The women were there to hold the space and to witness the birth, to honour it. The drumming was coming from outside the teepee and it was like the whole community was involved in the birth.

"So, the drumming was coming rhythmically and it was there to stimulate me as the baby into birth, to stimulate the contractions so that things would start to happen. It was a good feeling, like 'I want to be born, I want to be physical.'

"The drumming became more erotic, began to move around more, like a swaying and sensual dance. It was very welcoming and very sexual. Again, it was all inducive to being born, making the process happen. It was wonderful to be born with that feeling instead of being born induced with drugs as happened in my present life. Instead of being 'clinically' born, it was a totally conscious birth, from the mother's point of view, the people around, and me as the baby too. The drumming was joining where you come from with the physical in a good way so there was no fear, no desire not to be born.

"Then the drumming started to get faster and faster and it was bringing it nearer and nearer to the climax of the birth. I was thinking, 'It's nearly time to be born' [repeating it six months later, the excitement was still in his voice] and then I started to clear stuff from my present birth about not wanting to come out. I was able to relax and go with it, to get into a joyful state. I didn't feel pressurized to come out, unlike I had this life. Then when I felt right to come out, I came out.

42   "I kept my eyes shut and gave thanks to the temple. Then I just felt my way around the wall until I found the end of the snake and followed the snake out. I was conscious of the symbolism, that I was being born and releasing any resistance. I was becoming more and more joyous and seeing how helpful this was going to be for clearing patterns. When I came out it was dusk, which was interesting because I was born at dusk in my present life.

"I came out and opened my eyes. The most incredible thing was Augustine [the shaman] standing there waiting for me, grinning. I hadn't seen him animated before. He had this purple flower for me. It was just like, wow [opening up with his hands] this incredible welcome. It totally opened my heart. I knew he knew what had happened. It was an incredible moment. I'll never, never forget that. That for me is where I was born."

I asked Tim how the experience had affected him:

"It made me more able to take life on and make life happen. I no longer drift. There is a sense of trust, trust that is just natural. It helped me to manifest what I want in a clear way. I am still grounding the experience because that was a different world. It's a learning process. Now I am bringing it into my body and that will manifest in all sorts of different ways.

"It has helped with my parents as well, something that in the past would get to me, although I still feel it fleetingly, doesn't cause me to react. We are communicating much better. I can see them more clearly. It is good to be with them now. It is like coming home."

The following is the verbatim memory of a client some six months after the sessions. It illustrates how strongly the memory stays in the mind:

"My presenting problem was an uncomfortable sensation in my chest whenever someone praised me. It is quite common for people to feel embarrassed sometimes when they are being complimented. It can be uncomfortable when someone 'loves you more than you love yourself'. But this was different.

"The therapist asked me to remember the last time I had experienced the feeling in my chest that I was concerned about. I told him it was about a week ago and described the circumstances, what was said and how I felt. He then asked me to describe certain details and to be aware of the precise moment when I noticed the feeling. I described the feeling in my chest, discomfort in my upper chest, and how it became stronger and uncomfortable.

"The therapist explained that there may have been some experience in the past which had created the feeling in the first place and that this may have been an appropriate feeling at that time. But we agreed that it was not appropriate to feel this discomfort merely because someone was praising me. He took me into hypnosis and regressed me to the first time that I had experienced the feeling. We had not discussed past lives, only that there may have been some experience in the past that had created the feeling.

"Suddenly, I am in the countryside, there is a feeling of tension and fear. Shouting and anger. I am being killed, a spear through my chest. I am falling, sliding down a bank into a stream.

"We run the scene again. This time more slowly. We are North American Indians. There is a battle. I am being killed by a member of my tribe. Why? I am feeling very confused at this point. Why was I being killed by my own tribe?

"The therapist then suggested that I would now realize the significance of the events. It all became clear. We (the women and children) were being killed by our own tribe so that the enemy could not capture us. They did not kill me because I had done something wrong but because they loved me and were protecting me from a 'fate worse than death'.

"I realized that the feelings in my chest when I was being praised were linked to this experience. The spear through the chest, death – but from love not hatred.

"Once this had become apparent, the therapist asked me if I needed the feeling anymore. Certainly not!

"At our next session I reported that I had not had the feeling in my chest since the regression. The therapist took me back again to the same scene. The memories were the same but this time I was free from the emotion."

She never experienced the pain again.

GUIDED IMAGERY

In the following guided imagery example, the client was taking part in a workshop with me. She booked a regression session for the preceding day as she felt "something needs to be opened up first." As the regression progressed, Clarissa moved from observing to taking part:

"I can see this man. He's dressed in a shirt and breeches. He's standing by the side of the road, it's only a dirt track. It goes through the village, a miserable place, the houses are very poor. Oh, now a carriage is coming. It's being driven much too fast. It's that young fool. He acts like he owns the road.

"The man is hanging onto the back of the carriage, he's being carried along on it … He's running away …

"Now look, the man is under the wheels. The carriage has driven on, it didn't stop. He wouldn't care. The man is lying at the side of the road like a bit of old rag cast aside."

It was not clear to me whether she was the man, or an onlooker. I can usually get a good sense of the scene immediately, but this was confused. So I asked her where she was, was she that man in the road? She was a bit confused about this herself initially:

"No, I don't think so, I'm looking down on him. Oh, now he's gone, it's the same place but he's not there. I'm behind a tree, watching. Nat's with me. He's not as well to do as me, his clothes are rougher, dirty. But he's my friend, we do the work together."

Suddenly, her breathing changes, her manner becomes anxious, her voice much higher:

"Now I'm running, we're running. [panting] Through the trees, they catch at my clothes. Nat's ok, he's getting away. They're after me. It's the soldiers, they knew I was there watching. Got to get away …

"Now they've got us. They've tied us to a tree. Look at them, the bastards, they just do what they are told. They don't care about anything. They're taunting me now, saying I'm no better than I should be. But I won't let them know how I feel, I won't show them any emotion. You have to be strong when faced with people like this, they're so ignorant and they abuse their position … Aaaah. Bastards. No one will ever do that to me again."

I asked her what had happened:

"One of them stepped up and killed me. No warning. I was stabbed in the chest. Now I'm dead and they've gone away and left Nat there. I can't talk to him anymore, he's my friend and I can't talk to him."

I asked her if she knew why she'd been killed:

"I was accused of spreading sedition. I was trying to make things better for the people. Trying to break some of the power the aristocracy had. The peasants were starving, living in those

hovels. They couldn't do anything without permission. I wanted them to have some rights, I believed it was wrong to treat people like that. But I was an aristocrat myself and my own class misunderstood, they thought I wanted a revolution. So they set the soldiers on me and they killed me. I think they were exceeding their authority, but it was too late."

With Clarissa still in the after-death state as a man, we removed the knife from her chest and healed the wound. One of the things he was most concerned about was his friend, Nat. He seemed unable to move on, part of him was stuck there. We 'reframed' the situation by having him move forward to meet Nat at the end of his life.

Having explored that life a little more with Clarissa, and established that, at this stage, she did not want to do any more work on healing it, I brought her out of the regression. I knew we would have all weekend to deal with the issues raised. To close the session, we did some 'de-briefing' to identify issues that were relevant to her present life.

One or two things had struck me forcibly. One was how cold her voice had been when she said, "I won't let them know how I feel, I won't show them any emotion." This turned out to be a powerful pattern in her present life. When Clarissa was in the police force, she rounded up a mob of football hooligans with the aid of a male colleague. She was the one who confronted them and told them to break it up. "They went away meek as lambs," she said. "My male colleague asked me afterwards if I'd been scared. I said no but really I was shitting myself. I couldn't let him know that." She had quite clearly carried that dying thought over to her present life.

Not surprisingly, she also carried a deep antipathy to people who pushed other people around simply because they were in authority: a situation she frequently met in the police force but was powerless to change. Not showing her feelings had a physical repercussion: she had been invalided out of the police suffering from a stress-related anxiety state. That anxiety manifested as a pain in her chest, exactly where she had been killed in the past life. I also felt that the 'false accusation' arising out of misunderstood motives could well be significant, and it too turned out to be a present life pattern.

That Clarissa found it hard at first to focus on who she was is quite a usual occurrence. Levels of regression change. She started out at a light one and moved into a much deeper one. But it also threw up the question of whether that body in the road was real. When we explored it a little more, we felt that it may well have been what she feared would happen to her friend, a fantasy, rather than what actually did happen. She did not feel anything when he went under the wheels, but the sensation of running through the trees and what followed was all too real.

BODYWORK

Bodywork may well be part of a past life technique, but equally it can 'accidentally' trigger a past life memory if this is relevant to the condition being worked on.

Many years ago, I was working on a client using the metamorphic technique (a gentler version of reflexology which works on the spiritual level of being as well as the physical). The client had come for spiritual healing for a lump on his neck. Having given him hands-on healing to his neck, I felt compelled to work on his feet. Working from the top of the big toe down to the heel symbolizes coming into incarnation, down into physical matter. As I progressed down his foot, massaging the edge with my thumb, he was elated, laughing. As I neared his heel, he began to sob. Then he began to lash out with his foot, kicking against my hands. I used a pillow to allow him to go on kicking. All he could say was, "No, no, I don't want to, it's not time yet."

It became clear that he had somehow become pulled into incarnation, trapped against his wishes. Then, his birth had been induced. He was not ready to be born. Eventually he was pulled out by forceps only to be put in an incubator. While he was still in the spiritual world, he was "thinking about incarnating again but was undecided. Somehow it was not time."

Then, quite suddenly he flipped back into his last death. Again, it was not time. He was being beaten and killed. He felt cheated of life, but could not lash out at his attackers. Nor could he make them listen. He suddenly flipped out of his body 'into the light'. Here he was happy. He refused to look at his past life, but part of him remained stuck there feeling helpless. That part was saying: "It's no use protesting, they won't hear me. I cannot do anything about this." Not surprisingly, that thought manifested as the lump on his neck – right at the spot where one of the boots that had been kicking him caught him in the neck.

He needed to lash out with his feet, to kick away what held him. Eventually, he was able to reflect tranquilly on coming back into incarnation. We worked first on healing his etheric blueprint. He rubbed out the lump. Then, working down his foot, I took him through conception and birth, allowing him to take his own time about it; and then moved forward through his life to the present moment, healing as we went.

As he got up to the present moment, he said he could feel the lump on his neck getting hotter and hotter. It was spitting, "like frying a hamburger," and shrinking all the time. Soon it was gone. Some weeks later, all physical trace had disappeared.

Soul retrieval may be carried out as a separate end in itself, or it may form part of other regression work.

In the following example, the woman concerned had already explored a particular life in great detail. It had been causing her considerable problems in her present life as she had a close involvement with the house she had lived in during that past life. She thought it 'had been dealt with' because it had given her great insight into her present experiences. These insights had brought about change. But, when she undertook a regression for another purpose, that life popped up again:

"I'm back in the house again. I feel a bit funny. I keep walking round but no one will talk to me, no one seems to see me. I'm moving around a lot, I don't seem to walk there, one minute I'm in one room, then I'm somewhere else entirely. I can't find my room and there's no one to help me. Everyone looks different, the children are much older. Albert has gone, I can't find him anywhere. I don't know what I'm doing here. I'm so lost."

It became clear that she had gone back to a time after she had died in the house, but before she had moved on. Certain things kept her attached. She was rather like a ghost, but she had conscious awareness. Asked if there was anyone there in the between life state to help her she said:

"My guide's come to find me. He's taking me up into this light. It's very bright. It's nice here, I like it better. I'm being healed. He says I have to go forward in time, that I've got left behind. We're moving forward extremely quickly. Oh, there's another me waiting. It's me before I was born. She's coming forward to give me a hug. [Her physical body jerks as though from an electric shock.] Oh that's better, we're one now. Now I can be born. I'll be whole again. We're going into the womb ..."

She commented later that she felt like she'd always had a piece missing and it had come back to her. The experience changed her life. She became the person she was meant to be. When I checked with her recently, she said, "I am enjoying life so much more now that I am fully me."

Interestingly, a friend of hers had actually picked up a 'ghost' at the house. Following the final regression, the 'ghost' disappeared and was not seen again.

HOW DO SOULS REINCARNATE?

No one knows for sure just how people reincarnate, but we do have some clues and can make an educated guess. What's more, we can turn to the ancient religions for clarification, particularly as to why people should choose to reincarnate and how past life memories can be carried over from life to life. In the East, people are perceived to be on a journey, an eternal round of cause and effect. They progress by right action, and fall back by wrong action or inaction. They are perceived as having little choice in the matter: they are meeting their karma. However, regression to the between life state seems to indicate that choice may be involved. Quite simply, we are here to learn and to progress spiritually and we choose the conditions of our life accordingly.

The ancient Hindu scripture, the Bhagavad-Gita, tells us that Krishna states:

> The man whose devotion has been broken off by death goeth to the regions of the righteous, where he dwells for an immensity of years and is then born again on earth in a pure and fortunate family, or even in the family of those who are spiritually illuminated … from that time he struggles more diligently towards perfection…
>
> TRANSLATED BY WILLIAM Q JUDGE

Karmic Laws

Desire: we manifest/create what we want/need for this
incarnation.
Purpose: what we are here for. This can override desire.
Grace: an offer we can't refuse from our higher self to let
go of karma.

TYPES OF KARMA

Retributive: the boomerang effect, e.g. an eye for an eye.

Organic: old abuse of body, injuries, etc create dis-ease.

Attitudinal: old attitudes create present circumstances
including chronic illness.

Symbolic: present life conditions symbolize the past, e.g. a
bed wetter had been a witch ducker.

Mockery: deprecating other people's right to evolve in the
way that is right for them.

Suspension: not being dealt with this time round.

In the making: what is set in motion now.

Repeating patterns: the treadmill.

Phobias: constantly reliving fears arising from old
experience.

'Sins of omission and commission': what we have done
or felt (lust, greed, etc), or have failed to do that we
needed to do.

Vocational: continuation of previous work.

Technological: carry-over of ethical choices, etc, concerning
the use of technology for good or ill.

Grace: once you have done all you can, you can let go of it.

Merit: the things you got right of which you can reap
the benefit.

Redemptive: making reparation, sacrifice, clearing
collective karma.

Recompense: something which is 'owed' from the past.

Relationship: karma arising from past relationships or
emotional patterns.

Family karma: genetic or inherited patterns passing through
the family.

WHY DO PEOPLE INCARNATE?

The most usual reason for reincarnating to emerge from regression is to deal with 'unfinished business'. To right a wrong, make recompense and reparation, complete a lesson or a task, continue a relationship or a vocation, fulfil a promise. The second most common reason is to grow spiritually, to continue learning and developing. Some spiritually evolved souls return because they want to be of service; less evolved souls may have no choice. They are caught on an endless wheel of action and reaction, mindlessly doing what they have always done. In other cases, incarnation may be a way of hiding the truth about ourselves, both from oneself and others. Beyond the physical, everything is visible, known. Unpalatable 'facts' about ourselves can only be disguised whilst in incarnation.

HOW IS IT POSSIBLE TO HAVE
MEMORIES OF OTHER LIVES?

To understand how it may be possible to have memories of other lives, we must look at precisely what it is that remembers. Scientists would say that memory is a function of the brain. But is it? It seems to be more a function of mind, and mind, unlike the brain, is almost certainly non-physical as we shall see. And, in any case, is the brain located solely in the skull? Well, the

answer to this last question is no. Scientists have found brain cells in other parts of the body, the base of the spine for example. So, it may well be that even if memory is a brain function, it is not confined to the head. It is part of our overall consciousness. Nor, as anyone who has had a near death or out of body experience will tell you, are memory and consciousness confined to the body itself.

Near Death Experience

A brush with death. People who have a near death experience are, to all outward signs, dead. However, their consciousness continues. They are able to describe the scene later: a man who was blind could see and describe clearly the medical procedures being carried out, for example. However, they also experience a series of classic 'stages' as they move away from their body:

1 Leaving or hovering above the body.
2 Entering a 'tunnel'.
3 Moving towards a bright light.
4 Meeting a relative or guide figure.
5 A 'Life Review'.
6 The decision to return.
7 Loss of fear of death.
8 Awakening back in the body.

Out of Body Experience

An out of body experience often, but not always, happens when someone is sleeping. The physical body is left behind and conscious awareness goes travelling. The subtle body is, however, connected to the physical body by a 'cord' or strand of light of which the traveller may, or may not, be aware (this cord is severed at death).

An OOBE may be induced voluntarily or occur involuntarily during dreams, etc. The person will often see their physical body lying on the bed or sitting in the chair.

In scientific experiments, items were placed on top of high cupboards in rooms well away from where the 'travellers' were relaxing or meditating. Having consciously induced an out of body state, they were able to 'leave their body', travel to the place where the object was hidden, identify it and report back to the experimenters.

If regressions to, and spontaneous memories of, conception and the interuterine state are to be believed – and there is compelling evidence to say that they should be – then consciousness can certainly exist independently of the brain. Memories exist from a time when the foetus did not have a brain at all. People are able to describe the events surrounding their conception with great detail and clarity, including the feelings of their parents at the time. These invariably include details which have never been discussed within the family, and which can profoundly shock a parent when later confronted with the truth. They cannot understand where the child obtained this information: "I've never told anyone about that, it's always been my secret" is a common response. Parents too will often tell their children: "When you were little you talked about another family, another place. You seemed to have memories that did not belong to this life, but you forgot about it as you grew up." This is extremely common, children's memories of other lives have been studied for years as evidence for reincarnation, as we shall see.

There is undoubtedly, however, a 'physical location' in the brain that appears to store past life memories. This is, as might be expected, in the most ancient part of the brain. If the bony ridge at the base of the skull is massaged, it aids past life recall. If stimulated electrically, it throws up memories, often in the form of emotions such as fear or terror. This is clearly one of the places we store our 'old tapes'. Some researchers have argued that, simply because everyone's brain, if stimulated, comes up with these memories, there is no validity to the memories. They see the fear or whatever as a product of stimulating that particular part of the brain, rather than saying that the brain is storing a memory of fear in that spot *because that is where brains store such memories*. I would argue that it is this universality of past life memories stored in a specific part of the brain that indicates that they are likely to be true.

Nevertheless, the body itself appears to have its own memory: buried traumas and dramas can be triggered during massage, reflexology and other body-based therapies. Old emotions surface, tension is released. Massaging a shoulder, for instance, can trigger a childhood memory of being hit there. Such traumatic memories do not only relate to present life experiences. That same shoulder may have been wounded in battle in an earlier life and that may be the memory that is brought to the surface by the massage: 'a flashback'. So, it appears that something other than the physical body, which only exists during the present life, carries the memory. Which then leads us to ask what carries memories from life to life?

Eastern philosophies have much more subtle explanations for life than does the materialistically based western world. In particular, they see 'mind' as having a much more universal, all-embracing function of organization than the western concept of mind as a product of the brain. Whilst most western religions may acknowledge that we have a 'soul' which continues after death, few see that soul as being in existence before conception. The western world, nowadays, pays more attention to the psyche than to the soul. The psyche pertains to our inner life, but for many people that inner life is psycho-analytic rather than soul-based. The soul, it would appear, has little to do with everyday life. Physicians, the original 'healers of souls', have even less to do with the spiritual dimension of humankind.

In the East, however, there is no division. Man, and woman, is a spiritual being. That spiritual being comprises various subtle bodies as well as the physical body. Names for, and functions of, the various parts differ according to the philosophy, which can be confusing, but the basic concept can help us to understand how it is possible for consciousness to reincarnate. Some of the Eastern philosophies posit a 'permanent mental atom', an actual molecule of matter which passes from body to body. Others see it as 'aggregates', subtle parts that pass across matter. In some views, there is a single entity that passes from body to body. In others, there is no single entity, consciousness can divide and incarnate in a number of bodies.

EGYPT

In ancient Egypt, the only civilization other than Tibetan to have extensively mapped the far side of death, the physical body (the Kha) was only one part of a totality of being. Among the several subtle bodies was the Ba, often translated as soul or

spirit, but in actuality the animating principle or divine spark underlying life – pure spirit being Akh, the source of all life. It is the Ba which solidifies spirit into form. So we could look on it as a kind of etheric blueprint. It is the spiritual manifestation whilst the person is alive on earth, and the distilled essence of all that a person was, when deceased. When the Ba departed the body, the body died but the Ba was immortal and eternal, carrying with it the fullness of a person's individuality. In Egyptian art, the Ba is often depicted as a man-headed bird. It can leave the tomb at will and traverse the realms beyond death. The so-called Books of the Dead inscribed on the tomb walls are instruction manuals for the soul after death, a guide-book to the afterlife, as it were.

However, the Ba as spiritual essence is beyond the purely personal. The Ba needed something else to fix it into individual incarnation. This is the Ka, again often translated as soul but perhaps best known as 'the double'. This Ka is the pervading sense of individuality or 'I' that creates a personality during incarnation. It is, however, more than the ego. The Ka has 'tendencies' or impulses towards being and acting in a particular way: we could see it as potential being. It is magnetic, imprinted with all the experiences of a lifetime. After death, the Ka lived on in the tomb but could reincarnate, taking the imprinted memories into a new Kha (body). It was the unsatisfied desires or unlived impulses of the Ka which pulled the soul back into incarnation.

If a Ka had been divested of all its 'virtue', its human and spiritual qualities, then it degenerated after death to the point where it could not incarnate again in human form and passed into animal or vegetable life: a fate much feared by the ancient Egyptians as individuality was extinguished.

The Ba could reincarnate but not in the strictly personal sense. As an animating principle, it activated the body (the Kha) but did not imprint memories of specific individual lives. It was an overall plan of the more impersonal Higher Self, not the 'everyday self' of incarnation.

So, it is the Ka that we must look to for an explanation of how past life memories arise. It had three parts, the first an 'animal' or lower level Ka concerned with desires. When this was the most powerful part of the personality, the Ka would be drawn back into incarnation by unsatisfied desires or subtle addictions. This is the 'soul on a treadmill' Ka. The divine Ka heeded the call to spiritually evolve, so when this Ka was in the ascendancy, the reason for incarnating would be to perfect the self, the divine spark becoming conscious of itself. The 'intermediate' Ka served the spiritual self but acted as a go-between, mediating between the desires of the 'higher' and 'lower' natures. When this Ka incarnated most strongly, it would have both lessons to learn and ingrained desires to overcome.

Hieroglyphs show the creator-god Ptah, or his ram-headed equivalent Khnum, fashioning this 'etheric double' on his potter's wheel, often in the form of an upraised pair of forearms (symbol for the Ka). Sometimes the Ba hovers over it. Khnum is a form of Ba, he is the 'cosmic soul' animating all beings subject to cyclic rebirth. The Ba and the Ka together create the physical body (the Kha), imbuing it with spiritual essence and imprinting the memories from past lives at a subtle level. In the Birth Chamber of Luxor Temple, Khnum fashions the double bodies of the pharaoh. One of the doubles, the Ka, holds in his hand the Ba in the form of a heron.

We could look at this as the Ba (or Higher Self) creating the physical vehicle (the Kha), imbuing it with life at conception and the individual personality (the Ka) manifesting at the first breath.

At death, the reverse process, the Ba hovers over the mummy as the spiritual essence leaves the body. Once the spiritual essence has gone, the Ka has to follow as it cannot keep the body

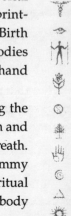

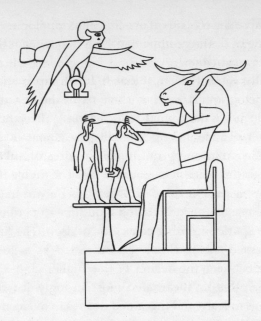

Khnum creating the etheric doubles on his potter's wheel
with the Ba hovering overhead

functioning. In the tomb we also often see paintings of the shadow, yet another subtle body, inhabiting this netherworld with the Ka and the Ba. Much of the Egyptian funerary arrangements were concerned with helping the Ba to pass on its way, propitiating the Ka until such time as it again took physical form.

The Ba and the Ka passed into Middle Eastern religions, including Christian, Jewish and Moslem, as the soul: an entity that animates the physical body whilst it is alive and leaves at death.

SUBTLE ENERGY BODIES

Open minded western scientists are investigating the concept of subtle energy bodies. (Russia is way ahead of the West in this field.) One of the tools they use is Kirlian photography. A Kirlian photograph, the product of a high frequency electric field, shows a corona of energy around living beings. It shows the corona in its entirety even if the physical part is missing. If a Kirlian photograph is made of a leaf, for example, and then half the leaf cut away, the next photograph will still show the energy corona around the whole leaf. We can therefore suppose that it shows the subtle energy body that surrounds and interpenetrates the leaf. Sensitive people, or psychics, can see this energy field (often referred to as the aura but sometimes known as the etheric or astral body). This energy field holds a great deal of information: well-being or disease, emotional states, mental attitudes, and, to some people's eyes, past lives.

The aura is made up of different 'layers': physical, emotional, mental and spiritual. They appear as layers of coloured light or swirling clouds of energy. Any blockage of the energies, or disease, will be visible in the relevant layer and will have consequences on other levels. A past life burden weighing down the shoulder on the emotional level will manifest physically in the present life as a frozen shoulder or upper back or neck pain. A blockage on the spiritual level, 'I cannot move forward', will manifest in the mental level as the thought 'I am stuck', in the emotional level as despair, and in the physical level as hip or knee problems.

Illness, or dis-ease, will, to a psychic eye, show up as a discolouration in the subtle body long before it manifests in the physical body. From this, we can assume that it is the subtle bodies that affect the physical level of being rather than the other way round. We can picture this as an 'etheric blueprint' that holds the thoughts, feelings and experiences of this and other lives. Rigid attitudes, persistent thoughts, painful emotions, etc, which register in those subtle bodies, have an effect on our physical well-being. We suffer from dis-ease or illness. Even

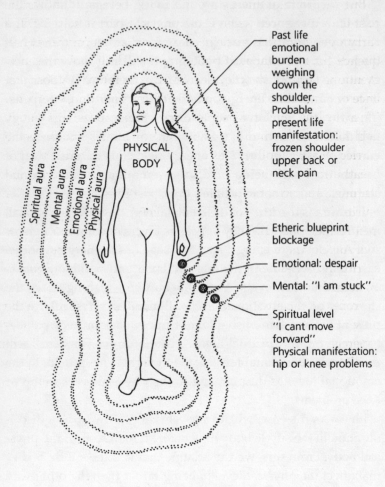

Past life emotional burden weighing down the shoulder. Probable present life manifestation: frozen shoulder upper back or neck pain

Etheric blueprint blockage

Emotional: despair

Mental: "I am stuck"

Spiritual level "I cant move forward" Physical manifestation: hip or knee problems

PHYSICAL BODY

Spiritual aura

Mental aura

Emotional aura

Physical aura

The aura with past life blockages

PRINCIPLES OF PAST LIFE THERAPY

our materialistic western medicine recognizes the concept of psychosomatic disease.

But we can take this a stage further. We can say that certain past life experiences will register on the 'etheric blueprint' and carry over from that past life a physical or emotional consequence. So, for instance, if we look at the elderly asthmatic lady mentioned earlier, she previously died with the physical experience of having the life crushed out of her, literally gasping her life away; the emotional sensation of being suffocated by guilt, and the mental thought: "I deserve this". Her 'etheric blueprint' carried the physical imprint of the chest injury, the difficulty in breathing; the emotional imprint of guilt and suffocation, and the mental imprint of the thought: "I have to pay for this". Her spiritual 'etheric blueprint' carried the desire to make reparation for the suffering she had caused to other people in that life. As a result, her physical body manifested asthma and her spiritual abilities helped her to heal other people and, ultimately, herself.

From half a century and more of regression therapy, we can now recognize that certain parts of the body carry particular repercussions from past life thoughts and experiences. These will be visible in the etheric blueprint.

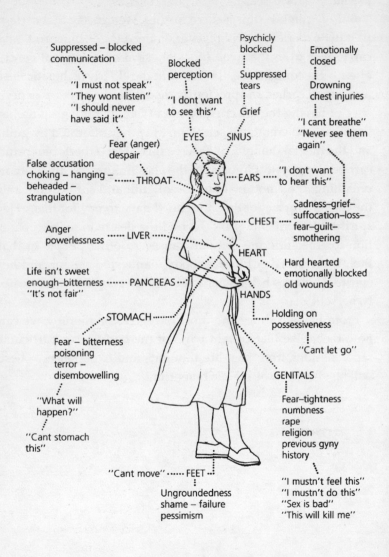

Suppressed – blocked
communication

"I must not speak"
"They wont listen"
"I should never
have said it"

Fear (anger)
despair

False accusation
choking – hanging –
beheaded –
strangulation

Anger
powerlessness

Life isn't sweet
enough–bitterness
"It's not fair"

Fear – bitterness
poisoning
terror –
disembowelling

"What will
happen?"

"Cant stomach
this"

Blocked
perception

"I dont want
to see this"

EYES

Psychicly
blocked

Suppressed
tears

Grief

SINUS

Emotionally
closed

Drowning
chest injuries

"I cant breathe"
"Never see them
again"

THROAT

EARS

"I dont want
to hear this"

Sadness–grief–
suffocation–loss–
fear–guilt–
smothering

CHEST

LIVER

PANCREAS

HEART

HANDS

Hard hearted
emotionally blocked
old wounds

STOMACH

Holding on
possessiveness

"Cant let go"

GENITALS

Fear–tightness
numbness
rape
religion
previous gyny
history

"Cant move" FEET

Ungroundedness
shame – failure
pessimism

"I mustn't feel this"
"I mustn't do this"
"Sex is bad"
"This will kill me"

The etheric blueprint (after Roger Woolger)

PRINCIPLES OF PAST LIFE THERAPY

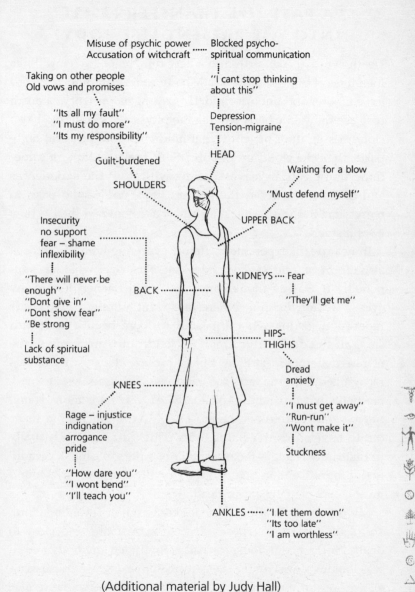

Misuse of psychic power
Accusation of witchcraft ·····

Blocked psycho-
spiritual communication

Taking on other people
Old vows and promises

"I cant stop thinking
about this"

"Its all my fault"
"I must do more"
"Its my responsibility"

Depression
Tension-migraine

Guilt-burdened

HEAD

SHOULDERS

Waiting for a blow

"Must defend myself"

UPPER BACK

Insecurity
no support
fear – shame
inflexibility

KIDNEYS ···· Fear

"There will never·be
enough"
"Dont give in"
"Dont show fear"
"Be strong

BACK ·····

"They'll get me"

HIPS-
THIGHS

Lack of spiritual
substance

Dread
anxiety

KNEES ·····

"I must get away"
"Run-run"
"Wont make it"

Rage – injustice
indignation
arrogance
pride

Stuckness

"How dare you"
"I wont bend"
"I'll teach you"

ANKLES ······ "I let them down"
"Its too late"
"I am worthless"

(Additional material by Judy Hall)

PRINCIPLES OF PAST LIFE THERAPY

HOW DOES THE RESIDUE FROM A PAST LIFE TRANSFER ITSELF INTO THE PRESENT LIFE BODY?

Death is rather like birth into a new dimension. A 'cord' links the physical body and the subtle body, just as an umbilical cord links mother and unborn child. If a psychic is present at a death they see the subtle body leaving the physical: "Gathering like a cloud, rising up. The 'cord' that holds it to the physical body parts, then the cloud moves off." So it looks as though something non-physical 'leaves', taking with it all the experiences and information about the present life. People who pass, in regression, to the afterlife state report a 'review' of the life they have just left.

In near death experiences, almost everyone who comes back also reports a 'Life Review', a looking back over what has happened: "It was as though my whole life flashed before my eyes." Acknowledging where one went wrong, what needs reparation, taking what appeared to have been a backward step, all the destructive emotions held onto, are some of the negative factors identified. But so too are the positive things recognized, all the acts of kindness, insights we gained, moments when we grew spiritually. And, what is more, sometimes what we think is the most negative thing we did turns out to have a positive value to us. This 'Life Review' usually dramatically changes the remainder of a person's life. It certainly did for me, and it included the past life reasons why I found myself experiencing a near death.

My own near death experience came when I was in labour. To all intents and purposes, I was unconscious and close to death. But my consciousness had actually left my body and 'I' was looking down on the scene from above. I saw a nurse casually glance at me and say: "It's unusual for someone to slee during this stage of labour – Oh, my God! Someone get the oxygen and fetch a doctor." Pandemonium was then let loose as they worked to bring me round and deliver the child.

Meanwhile, up on the ceiling, I was talking to a guide. He took me through my present life, with all its difficulties, and showed me that I had chosen to undergo these lessons. He helped me to identify certain spiritual tasks I had yet to undertake. He also showed me myself in labour in another life. But this was very different to the sterile conditions below me. I was in a miserable hut, lying on filthy straw, with a grimy old woman struggling to deliver the child, and surrounding me were a horde of equally dirty children. I died then simply because I could not face yet another child in these dreadful conditions. (Many years later, I met a man who said, "You were my mother and you died and left me," and who went on to describe the scene in minute detail.)

The guide said to me, "You opted out then, you are opting out now. But, if you opt out now, you will only have to do it all again. And there is your spiritual purpose to fulfil. The choice is yours." Above me was the tunnel and bright light that most people pass through in a near death experience, below me was my body and my child. The lure of the tunnel was seductive and strong, but I knew that if we were both to survive, I had to return to my body there and then. So, reluctantly, I found myself back in my body. The next six months were the low spot of my entire life as the old patterns disintegrated, but after that my life changed drastically. That experience was directly responsible for the work I now do.

So, if it changes us in our present life, we can surely assume that in a Life Review following death, the insights will be carried forward into the next life. Not only that, they will also link up with our previous death reviews.

THE STAGES OF DEATH

From reported experiences of regressions through death to the post-death state, we can roughly formulate the 'stages of death' (see illustration). These stages are best understood as a change in vibration. Each subtle level vibrates at a slightly higher frequency to the next, and so is not visible from the lower vibration state (except to someone who is highly sensitive). Each stage is a death of a layer of the subtle body and with it the experiences of that level of being. Sometimes it is necessary to re-experience the emotions, desires, etc, before they can be let go of. However, the core experiences and insights are carried forward to the next level. If these are negative patterns, they will manifest again and again in life after life until recognized consciously and detached from.

The Stages of Death

1 Subtle bodies leave the physical.
2 Passing through the tunnel.
3 Detach from the physical: cord severs.
4 The Life Review in which all old emotions are experienced.
5 Detach from the 'emotional' body.
6 Move into the 'astral' body. Live out unexperienced desires. The personality falls away.
7 Detach from desires.
8 Move into the 'mental' body. Review ideas, beliefs and constructs.
9 Detach from beliefs and ideals. Receive 'higher mind' teachings.
10 Move into the 'spiritual' body. Make meaningful choices that are not simply a repetition of karmic patterns.

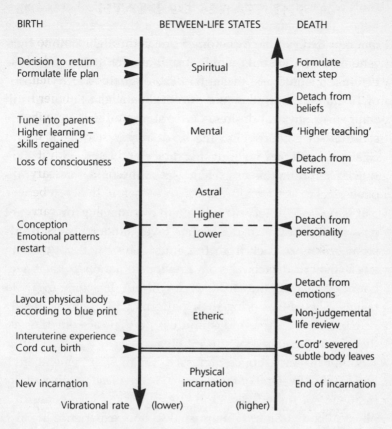

The Stages of Birth and Death

At levels 1 to 8, people tend to see what they expect to see. Visions of heaven or hell for instance, or even continuing to live life much as they lived it on earth. Desire rules these states. What we most desire, we will try to manifest. There is a wonderful story in one of the first modern accounts of a near death experience (in *Return from Tomorrow* by George Ritchie, now out of print) of being taken to the astral level of being and shown how this interacted with the physical realm. There were many

PRINCIPLES OF PAST LIFE THERAPY

souls who had not yet let go of their desire for alcohol and cigarettes. They 'haunted' pubs, to which they were drawn like
magnets. Every time a customer put down their pint or ciga-
rette, one of the souls would try to snatch it but of course
their hand would pass through it. These are the 'hungry ghosts'
of Tibetan Buddhism, or the 'Ka' of the ancient Egyptian still
trapped in physical desires. Other stories of the between life
state tell of places where the souls manifested alcohol and
cigarettes until they realized that they were no longer receiving
satisfaction from this use. Then, the soul would pass onto another level.

It is possible to incarnate again at any stage; people do not
pass automatically to the higher levels. Indeed, some souls
seem to bounce back from the etheric level without gaining
any insight or detaching from previous emotions. Others will
bounce back from the astral level, without detaching from old
beliefs. They either bring their patterns with them, endlessly
reacting to the same old stimulus; or they act out the last
thought they had in a significant life.

So, for instance, I once regressed a man who 'remembered'
hundreds of lives: all of them male. When questioned about the
frequency of these lives, he had said, "I just love being in a
physical body." Since it is unusual to only experience life as a
male, I asked if I could regress him. He agreed reluctantly but
said, "You won't find anything." As he went into the regression
he curled up in a foetal position, covering his eyes, ears and
mouth with his hands. "I'm not going to tell her about this," he
said. But tell me he did, although as he rushed off immediately
he came out of the regression it is doubtful that, to this day, he
knows that I know what went on.

He went back to being a young girl in a village in ancient
times. The village was invaded and s/he was raped repeatedly.
All she wished to do was die, but she lived. She felt great shame

PRINCIPLES OF PAST LIFE THERAPY

all through that life. As she died she said, "I will never be a
woman again." Immediately after death, his soul looked for
another body to inhabit, then another and another. All were
male. He never moved into the higher levels of the between life
state where he could have reconsidered that decision never to
be female again. Nor, during the regression, was he willing to
reconsider or to do any healing work on that young girl. So, the
pattern will no doubt repeat itself.

THE STAGES OF BIRTH

Assuming that one has passed to the 'higher' levels of the between life state, there comes a point when the decision is made
to return to earth. It becomes obvious that we need to enter into
physical experiences again. At this level, choice is a factor. We
formulate a life plan. We find the parents who will create the
right experiences, surroundings and emotional ambience that
we need, and possibly the necessary genetic inheritance too. If
the decision is made at any of the 'lower' levels, choice may not
be a factor, we will be pulled towards our old patterns and the
people with whom we have endlessly interacted.

At each stage of incarnation, we lose awareness of the stage
before but we bring the information we need coded into the
etheric blueprint and this can be reactivated at any time. American psychologist Stanislav Grof has found that during physical
birth, past life memories are activated. We re-experience our
past during the 'death' from the interuterine state to independent physical existence that we call birth.

The Stages of Birth

1 Decide to return.
2 Formulate life plan.
3 Choose parents, etc.
4 Leave the spiritual realms, taking spiritual imprint.
5 Move into the mental body. Receive 'higher teachings'.
6 Conception.
7 Move into astral body. Reconnect to old skills and emotions.
8 Move into etheric body. Organize the physical body from etheric blueprint.
9 Interuterine experience will activate old emotional and mental patterns.
10 New incarnation.

WHERE DID IT START?

This is a complex question and the answer given here must be viewed as symbolic rather than factual. It is clear from between life regression experience, that we simply do not have the necessary constructs to understand either the nature of spiritual life or that of time from our earthly perspective. Nor can we fully understand the purpose. But we can experience our own part in the process.

Souls, or spirits, can be seen as emerging from a 'pool' of spiritual essence, 'the Source', into which they will ultimately return (see illustration). The 'piece' of this spiritual essence which first emerges then divides (a soul group), and divides again as it journeys down through different levels of vibration until it reaches the earth plane (the densest level of vibration) as an

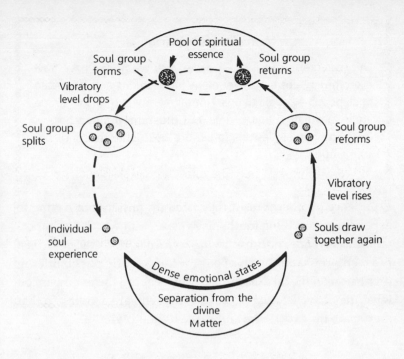

Pool of spiritual essence

Soul group forms

Soul group returns

Vibratory level drops

Soul group splits

Soul group reforms

Vibratory level rises

Individual soul experience

Souls draw together again

Dense emotional states

Separation from the divine
Matter

The soul's symbolic journey into matter

individual soul. Awareness of being an innately spiritual, divine being is, at this dense level of vibration, usually lost. The soul is deeply immersed in emotional experiences and old patterns.

Recognition of that inner spiritual element, and of other soul group members, starts the process of return and reunification. On the way back, soul groups may recombine sharing experiences. Eventually, all that has been experienced is taken back into the communal pool, which has its consciousness raised by the collective experience. Therefore, 'new' souls which then emerge do not, symbolically, have as far to 'fall' before return. And, what is more, it is possible for souls to 'borrow' the

Soul Groups

Our soul group consists of people with whom we have travelled throughout time, over many incarnations and interacted in all possible combinations. Not all members of a soul group are in incarnation at one time, but those people who help us learn the hardest lessons in life are usually members of our soul group.

experience of other souls if they need to, rather than having to experience everything for themselves: a point which has important implications for those trying to prove the veracity of past, life memories, and which opens up therapeutic possibilities in regression. In the Sufi teachings, souls leaving the earth pass on what they have learned to 'new' souls who are arriving so that they share the experience and make it their own.

PAST LIVES:
THE EVIDENCE

Nowadays reincarnation is seen largely as an Eastern belief. However, it is an ancient belief and one which was once widespread in the West. Greek philosophers, such as Plato, refer to it. Pythagoras said that he had formerly been Aethalides and was reborn as Euphorbus – who was wounded by Menalaus at the siege of Troy. In that life he said he had been given a gift from Mercury of the memory of his soul's transmigrations, and also the gift of recollecting what his own soul and the souls of others had experienced between death and rebirth. He also believed he had been a beautiful courtesan. Plato warned of the dangers of 'bad karma':

> Know that if you become worse you will go to the worse souls, or
> if better to the better … and in death you will do and suffer what
> like may fitly suffer at the hands of like (Laws).

Reincarnation was a basic precept in gnostic Christianity and appears in many of the 'banned' books of the New Testament – at a Council some two centuries after Christianity started, over 200 gospels were whittled down to just four 'acceptable' volumes. Even in these, some references to reincarnation remain (see Matthew 16:13 – 4, 17:9 –13, 11:11–15, John 9:34, Romans 9:10 –13,

Revelations 3:12). However, in 553 a Council of the Church rati-
fied the anathema of the Emperor Justinian against the Doctrine
of Origen concerning the pre-existence of the human soul and,
by implication, reincarnation.

An apocryphal story suggests that it was the Emperor's wife,
Theodosia, who insisted that reincarnation be done away with.
Apparently, she was afraid that she would have to pay for her
excesses in the present life at some future time! From this time
on, official belief in reincarnation in the Christian church ceased,
although several 'heretical' sects continued to follow this precept and it surfaced from time to time during the next 1500
years. The belief was 'revived' in the West by the Theosophists
and other esoteric movements.

So, what is the evidence for reincarnation?

There are five basic approaches to past lives:

1 'Prove it' – scientific – seek evidence.
2 'Disprove it' – find other explanations.
3 'Believe it' – religious – rely on doctrine.
4 'Read it' – psychic information.
5 'Experience it' – access subconscious or far memory to relive
   the past.

'PROVE IT'

In the 'prove it' method, evidence is sought that can be
checked out. There are serious, scientific researchers who
devote a great deal of time and meticulous inquiry to the subject of past lives. Much of the evidence for this work comes
from children's spontaneous memories. Memories that are
present almost from birth and which, therefore, are not conta-
minated by history lessons or what has been read in books.

Such memories are prized in cultures that accept reincarnation as part of their religious beliefs.

RESEARCH

A great many people undertake hypnotic regression to explore their past lives simply to get evidence that they have lived before. Some of this evidence is extremely persuasive. Indeed, there are magazines and many, many books dedicated to this approach who will say that they have proved that reincarnation exists beyond a doubt. Professor Ian Stevenson, one of the leading authorities, does not go this far but, having examined over 2500 'memories', he presents an ever increasing number of cases which he believes are 'suggestive of reincarnation'. Many of these cases are centred around Indian children and their memories of apparent past lives. In several instances they claimed to be the incarnation of men or women who had died recently, people who were traceable. On talking to the widows of these men, intimate details were confirmed of which the child could have no knowledge. Physical scarring or unusual birthmarks at the site of previous injuries is also a feature of reincarnation memories. It seems as though the 'etheric blueprint', in carrying a memory of the injury, creates a tangible reminder.

Professor Stevenson investigates spontaneously remembered past lives rather than induced memory – of which he is, on the whole, somewhat sceptical. Nevertheless, he does quote the case of Bridey Murphy as "stating details about life in Ireland during the first half of the 19th century that I do not believe she had learned normally." Talking about the much vaunted 'exposure' of the Bridey Murphy case as a fraud, Professor Stevenson comments: "Persons who dismiss this case as an instance of cryptomnesia are usually unaware of the exposure of the alleged exposure of the case."

This was one of the first 'past life memory' cases to hit the headlines.

Some forty years ago, an American housewife was hypnotically regressed to a life in Ireland as Bridget (Bridey) Kathleen Murphy (1798–1864). Speaking in an Irish brogue and using appropriate terminology, she gave a detailed account including place names and obscure information about such matters as holiday customs, currency, furnishings and clothes of the time. She could even dance an Irish jig and sing folk songs. She recollected buying groceries from a shopkeeper called John Carrigan and also shopping at Farrs. Both of these shops were traced as trading in Belfast at the time in question. She lived in a house called The Meadows, outside Cork, which appears on a contemporary map. She stated that her husband and father were barristers – a 'fact' much criticized by later commentators as it was prior to the Catholic Emancipation Act. However, although the majority of Catholics were not emancipated until 1825, a 1793 ruling specifically allowed Catholics to enter the legal profession.

A journalist, William J Barker, intensively researched the case in Ireland for three weeks. Although many details could not be proved due to lack of records, nothing she said was disproved. He concluded "Bridey's autobiography stands up fantastically well in the light of such hard-to-obtain facts as I did accumulate." He published 'The Truth about Bridey Murphy' which supported the case, although his name was used as a 'prosecution witness' in anti-Bridey articles.

The popular press mounted a concerted effort to debunk the Bridey story, perpetuating many inaccuracies in the process. They even claimed that the hypnotist, Morey Bernstein, had shamefacedly admitted to 'Hoaxing World with Search for Bridey Murphy', although in fact Bernstein made no such admission. The 'evidence against' mostly concerned 'witnesses' making statements about 'facts' that, on the whole, did not even appear in original transcripts of the regression. For example, a clergyman criticized the 'fact' that she described buying shoes and dresses when these things would have been hand-made. The only flaw was that Bridey had not mentioned buying clothing, whereas she did mention it being made for her. They also found people out of her (recent) past who, it was claimed, could have passed on Irish memories to the regressee. The flaw here, for example, was that her aunt (who did not in any case meet the regressee until she was 18) was claimed to be of Irish extraction but had in fact lived all her life in Chicago and could not have passed on Irish memories to her niece, as she did not have any.

Most people remember this case as a hoax. But CJ Ducasse, former chairman of the Department of Philosophy at Brown University, studied the case and concluded: "Neither the articles in magazines or newspapers, nor the comments of psychiatrists hostile to the reincarnation hypothesis have succeeded in disproving or even establishing a strong case against the possibility that many of the statements of the Bridey personality are genuine memories of an earlier life of Ruth Simmons [a pseudonym] over a century ago in Ireland."

FINDING 'EVIDENCE'

In my experience, people who are looking for evidence in order to be convinced of the validity of past lives, rarely find what they are seeking. For instance, a workshop participant felt let down when all he came up with were experiences that, whilst therapeutic, had, so far as he was concerned, no validity because he could not prove them. Some time later, having consulted a hypnotherapist, he rang me to say he had a great deal of 'evidence' including dates, the church where he was buried, the site of his grave, etc. He was rushing off to check. To his great disappointment, whilst the church was clearly there, he was not in either the records or the graveyard.

On the other hand, during my spontaneous regressions to other lives, various details have emerged which I have been able to confirm. One of my first pictures was of a group of people being pursued through trees by an armoured man on horseback. He had some foot soldiers with him. I was running with them through the woods, which were becoming increasingly dark. It was a partial eclipse of the sun. The darkness allowed us to escape as we knew the area well. I was given a place, date and time (unusual for me). When I checked with the Greenwich Observatory, there was a partial eclipse at that time on that day, visible from the place in question, which would have given that degree of darkness. I also sent a sketch of the armour to the College of Heralds, who were quite excited when they confirmed the details. French armour of that date is exceedingly rare. Unfortunately, I had to tell them the actual armour did not exist any more.

THE EVIDENCE: SIMON'S STORY

I have chosen to use Simon's story as an evidential example because it brings together several strands: early memories in the form of a recurring dream, family connections, and a continuation of an old occupation.

His experience began as a recurring dream when he was about 7 or 8 years old. The details of the dream stayed with him into adulthood. He has only to shut his eyes to see it again:

"The dream was of being in uniform, definitely camouflage uniform. Wearing a helmet, lots of kit all over, webbing, ammunition pouches, rucksack. The picture is of a large glider, and the back of the glider is open. It is empty inside and I am running round the glider.

"The dream would go from being a smooth black and white photo, to almost clear, then it would go very distorted as though someone moved the contrast button, very mishmashed.

"We were running round woods, a Northern European setting, leaves on the trees, a lot of emotional energy. And then, nothing.

"So that was about it, no distinct pattern to the thing. Always the glider, what I was wearing, a sense of panic, a sense of urgency, a sense of drama.

"It is very obvious what point of history we were at. It can't have been much prior to 1945 because no one ran around in camouflage at that stage, and it can't have been after then because of the gliders. We haven't used gliders since 1944–5 in a battle situation. So that focuses the time."

This is Simon's memory of the one and a half hour session some two years after it occurred:

"In the regression we went back to a wood initially. I was doing a lot of running around, in uniform, out looking for something – rescuing somebody – taking someone back. Lot of shouting, lot of noise, gunfire, everything was going on. Very graphic. It was at that point, whilst we were taking this chap, whoever he was, to safety, that I blanked out.

"Very clearly the uniform was there, what I was wearing, all very similar to the dream."

I took him back to a slightly earlier time to establish more detail of what was going on:

"There was a lot of waiting before we went in, the fog and mist, the fact that we were delayed, the boredom. We also covered the training, a trip to Palestine, my wife and child, but it was the waiting to go in, being delayed two or three days, that made the most impression. And then, going across in the glider. It seemed probable that I was at Arnhem, and that I went in by parachute."

82   Simon then started to research the 'facts' as he knew them.

"I knew about Miles Henry [a distant cousin], I had already discovered him in my family tree before I came for the regression. I didn't know much about him at that stage. I knew he had been a member of my greater family, he had been born in 1921, he had married and had a daughter, and he had been killed in action. I also knew where he had been buried. That was all.

"I went to the Parachute Museum and discovered that Miles Henry had been a Captain in 10 Para and again confirmed where he was buried in Holland. They said the only way I would get more information about how he was killed was through the 10 Para War Diaries which were in the Imperial War Museum. So I went to the War Museum Library. Had the diaries presented to me. Opened the diaries up. Found the reference to Miles Henry. It gave me huge tingles up and down my spine. He had been in Palestine, came back, was in training in 1944. He had gone in as Intelligence Officer of 10 Para at the Regimental Headquarters at Arnhem.

"He was killed with another guy trying to rescue a fellow who had been wounded, trying to take him back to an Aid Station. Miles Henry was wounded badly, and died of his wounds that night without regaining consciousness.

"The diaries confirmed that they had been held up by the fog for two or three days, they jumped, and had used gliders to come in."

Simon, an ex-army officer, is absolutely sure that this was his previous life:

"I just know it happened, I know it was me. I can't not believe it, there are too many pieces of the jigsaw that come together for it not to be believable."

However, there are people who are determined to prove otherwise. This is the 'disprove it' approach. They have alternative explanations, some of which are also extremely persuasive, but others, which require a certain degree of faith, cannot be backed up with hard evidence either.

PAST LIVES: ALTERNATIVE EXPLANATIONS

Brain disorders

The psychogene – family and racial memory

Paramnesia and false memory

Cryptomnesia – hidden memory from books, films, etc.

The collective unconscious – tuning into what has gone before

Possession by dead spirits

The power of suggestion

Psychiatric illness such as schizophrenia or Multiple Personality Disorder

Psychically reading a place

Brain disorders

As we have already seen, mind is a mysterious and elusive substance that refuses to be tied to the brain. We also know that mind can influence the body: stigmata is only one form of mind-induced physical phenomenon. I have seen scars on the wrists and ankles of people who 'remember' being crucified, birthmarks at the site of old burns, scars on old wound sites, and many other incidents. Under hypnosis, burn blisters may appear without physical heat being applied, blood loss can be stemmed and healing can be induced during surgery.

Notwithstanding, it is to the brain, rather than the mind, and especially to its disorders, that science looks for alternative explanations for apparent reincarnation memory and for physical manifestation. Dr Susan Blackmore, who is wheeled out on every British television programme where debunking of psychic phenomena is called for, investigated apparent past life memories. She visited a researcher in the States who stimulated parts of the brain with electrodes, producing fear and images of murder, etc. Dr Blackmore was clearly disturbed by what she 'saw' and felt during this experiment. Unfortunately for the interests of objective reporting, no one thought to ask her to describe in detail what actually happened – or if they did it was not included in the programme. 'Coincidentally', the point stimulated is where many past life therapists believe past life memories are stored, but the 'explanation' given was that the brain is an independent organism that *creates* such memories.

Brain disorders such as temporal lobe epilepsy are posited as accounting for spontaneous memories of other lives. Psychiatric disorders such as hysteria, schizophrenia and hypermanic states are also suggested. I have certainly seen apparent past life memories randomly 'breaking through' in these states but there is no evidence to support either the 'delusion' or 'actuality' hypothesis at this stage of our knowledge.

One complicated explanation of the phenomenon of 'déjà vu' is that the brain actually perceives a place ahead of conscious sight. When conscious awareness 'catches up', it feels like 'I've been here before'. However, this explanation does not account for someone being able to tell in detail what is around the next corner before they get there.

The psychogene
Many researchers believe in a 'psychogene'. The psychogene is non-physical, it is part of our psyche. As CG Jung said: "The body has an anatomical prehistory of millions of years, so also the psychic system." Just as our physical characteristics are

handed on through the combined DNA of our parents, so the family and ancestral memory right back to the remotest times passes through the psychogene.

The only problem with using the psychogene to explain past life memories, is that people have memories of lives that their ancestors could not possibly have lived. For instance, a young man who came to one of my workshops wanted to know why, this time around, he had been born in the West. All his other memories were of China, virtually up to the present day. He had no Chinese ancestry, certainly in the last three or four hundred years because the family tree had been checked. Similarly, young children who claim memories of other lives may not be related through blood ties, although some are. Tibetan lamas are now being reborn in the West into families which have no Tibetan blood.

Paramnesia and False Memory Syndrome

Psychologists and critics of past life memory often put paramnesia forward as an 'explanation' for reincarnation memories. Paramnesia is defined as 'the illusion of recognizing something that has never actually been part of one's previous experience'. It is somewhat akin to fantasizing. It may well account for the 'watching a film' type level of regression where although the story seems to be familiar, there is little feeling attached to it. The experience has, as it were, been 'plucked out of the ether'.

In false memory syndrome, a memory is induced, but it is not a true memory. This has hit the headlines recently in child abuse cases where hypnotherapists and others appear to have stimulated memories of abuse in childhood which did not actually occur. (This may relate to taking too literally something which is a symbolic analogy.) If the therapist is looking for abuse, then a memory of abuse may well surface. If looking for past lives, then these will arise. Most therapists use suggestions like "going back in time to before you were born," or "which will lead you to other lives."

People who are in a trance state are in a state of heightened suggestibility, which is why therapists have to be so careful about their use of language. It is very easy to implant suggestions. There is also some evidence that also, whilst in this state, the person undergoing the regression may be particularly anxious to please and will, unconsciously, 'make up' a story for the therapist. An experienced therapist can usually spot this, and will use the story to illuminate a present life problem rather than accepting it as incontrovertible, factual 'truth'.

One of the ways to check whether paramnesia is operating is to try to change the detail of a scene. If it is true memory, it will remain as seen (unless deliberately reframing it). If it is false, then details such as time period, characters, colours, sex, can all be changed. In the right hands, paramnesia can actually be quite therapeutic as it can 'reframe' a scenario in order to heal it.

Cryptomnesia

Cryptomnesia involves 'hidden memory' surfacing. Some 'debunking' of past life memories where the subject spontaneously spoke in a foreign language (xenogossis) has relied on the subject having had a nursemaid who spoke that particular language, for instance. As it was in early childhood, no conscious memory is retained. It is more difficult to use this as an explanation if the language is in its archaic form. Gina Germinera has documented a girl who spoke in ancient Coptic when hypnotically regressed and several of Professor Ian Stevenson's cases spoke foreign languages to which, as far as could be ascertained, neither they nor their families had access.

Cryptomnesia may lie behind some reincarnation memories. Most of us find ourselves drawn to certain periods in history, and ignore others. We read books or we watch films. We may have quite a wide knowledge of particular periods of history, especially if the writer had a good researcher. However, regressions often contradict accepted 'history'.

> Xenoglossis
> Speaking in a language, usually archaic, of which the subject has no conscious knowledge.

The collective unconscious

The collective unconscious is a pool of memory which contains all that has gone before, not only for our individual families or tribes, but for the whole of the human race. It is an imprint of everything that is, or was. It has been referred to as 'an incredible psychic computer'. Given the right access code, we can call up anything or anyone. If we tune into this source, we can remember, or re-live, any life that has previously been. It is similar to the concept of the Akashic Record. However, the collective unconscious is usually regarded as a part of our consciousness, indeed all our consciousnesses, whereas the Akashic Record is seen as something apart, a kind of universal consciousness to which we have access.

In the collective unconscious are all the stories of the human race, all the archetypes, all the 'plays' that are enacted over and over again with a cast of thousands, or one or two people. The actors may be different, the historical setting may change, but the essential stories remain the same. Each plays his allotted part. This may go a long way to explaining why so many people 'regress' to a particular figure or group experience. It may not be that they have actually been that person, or part of that group, but they may have played that part in the play somewhere along the line, and therefore it resonates with them.

Possession by dead spirits

Possession by dead spirits is an interesting proposition to put forward because it presupposes survival of bodily death. The theory is that the spirit communicates in a way which makes the life seem like the regressee's. When I first had my spontaneous past life memories, the medium who was running the development circle I was sitting in said, "That's nice, dear, the guides are showing you where they lived." He did not believe in reincarnation. I could not understand why these places and events were so very familiar to me, they felt like 'home'. It was only when I met Christine Hartley that the idea that they could be 'my' memories made everything drop into place.

However, I regressed a guy, Larry, in the States who constantly felt that he was being called upon to live out some great purpose. He did not know what it was, nor did he, in some strange way, actually believe it was his purpose. When we regressed him, we went back to an unfinished life. Eventually, though, it became clear that it was not 'his' life. He referred constantly to his dead father and I questioned him closely about this as I felt there was something about the reliving that did not ring true. It emerged that his father, who had died young, was trying to take over and live out his unlived life through his son. The 'past life memory' was another life in which the father had died young. We needed to negotiate with his father, to cut the ties and to persuade him to move on, to enable him to see that his life was indeed complete here on earth this time around and that he needed to progress 'on the other side'. We did several other sessions, and eventually Larry was able to let his father go and then tune into his own purpose in incarnating – something very different from what he had been trying to live out for his father. By the end of the month, it was as though a different person was in the room. Larry even looked different.

The power of suggestion

The power of suggestion is extremely strong. Suggest to some-one that they are seeing, or feeling, something graphic, and it is almost certain they will join in with that suggestion, particular-ly if they are in a relaxed state. Some people are resistant, just as some people cannot be hypnotized. But, on the whole, the power of suggestion is something to watch out for when under-going regression. Most past life therapists are highly aware of this power, almost all of us use it at some time in our sessions – not to induce false memory but to initiate healing. It is what dif-ferentiates therapy from simply 'reliving'.

Psychiatric illness

Multiple Personality Disorder is a recognized psychiatric 'ill-ness'. Apparent past life memories are often dismissed by psy-chiatrists and psychologists as forming part of this syndrome.

In Multiple Personality, a part, or parts, of the overall person-ality becomes split off. (This is usually, but not necessarily, a response to childhood trauma or severe abuse.) So, the multiple personalities are viewed as split-off parts of the same disor-dered subconscious mind housed within the 'host body'.

This split-off part re-emerges later as a separate entity with his or her own distinct persona and memories. Such re-emer-gence is often triggered by hypnosis or severe stress or depres-sion, although it may occur spontaneously. The personality may, or may not, be aware of the other personalities seemingly inhabiting the same host body, and can present as pertaining purely to the present time or as belonging to a past era. There may be a central, organizing personality who controls the pro-cess, or there may be a multitude of personalities fighting to be heard.

Psychology views all such personalities as necessarily being laid down, or split off, at a very early age in the present life. The

phenomenon must, therefore, include para- or cryptomnesia – presumably also from early infancy unless the personality incorporates new material as the host body matures. To explain the apparent past life personae which are often a feature of Multiple Personality, psychologists or psychiatrists invariably rely on external early life figures, such as nursemaids, grandparents or neighbours, who tell the child stories which then re-emerge as 'memories' of actual personal experience. It is, of course, also possible that the past life personality was brought in complete at birth and lay dormant until activated. Or, it could be a separate deceased person taking over (the 'possession by dead spirits' approach).

There would, however, appear to be a definite distinction between true Multiple Personality and the past life memories that surface during a regression. The past life persona only appears when induced. It does not have an autonomous life of its own, nor does it come and go at will, as happens in Multiple Personality. In a Multiple Personality case, one of several personalities seemingly housed in a middle-aged woman claimed to have lived 200 years previously. She did not, however, claim that she had reincarnated into the present body. She maintained that she was a separate person who happened, at this time, to be housed within the host body for a specific purpose. Past life memories present as reliving a previous incarnation in another body: a life which is separate and distinct from the present one.

Multiple Personality can only be termed absolutely as a disorder of the mind if it is viewed as an undeniable psychopathology (psychiatric disease). It could be viewed as an expansion of consciousness into a multi-faceted awareness that incorporates the experiences of personalities from other lives, or different dimensions of being.

This explanation presupposes that people have an ability to tune into places, using extra-sensory perception. The place then tells them what has happened there. This is a bit like seeing a ghost. It can account for some déjà vu memories. However, for aother than where the reader is situated, we must assume that this ability is not limited by time and space.

'BELIEVE IT'

The third approach to past lives is one that millions of people adopt: the 'believe it' or religious stance. For these believers in reincarnation, no proof is necessary. Virtually all the religious or philosophical doctrines of the East hold reincarnation as one of their fundamental truths. What is more, as we have seen, it was not a totally foreign concept in the West. Most of the so-called 'native' beliefs of North and South America, Australia, Africa and the South Seas, all look to a cycle of rebirth. It seems to be one of man's fundamental impulses.

TIBET

Tibet must be the only country in the world where the nominal head of government (Tibet has a 'government in exile') receives his authority because he is the incarnation of himself fourteen times over.

In Tibetan Buddhism, where reincarnation is taken for grant-ed, the high lamas are all recognized as reincarnations of them-selves in an unbroken line stretching back hundreds of years. When a lama died, preparations were at once made to seek out his next incarnation. He had often given clues as to where he would reincarnate. The Oracle was consulted, senior lamas set out to scour the land. Typically, the child was about four or five whcn 'found'. Tests were administered, including picking out

his own possessions from amongst others, and only when the lamas were satisfied was the new incarnation recognized and installed. The process is much more difficult now that the majority of Tibetans live in a Chinese occupied country.

When the present Dalai Lama, the fourteenth of his line and both spiritual and secular leader of his people, was 'found', he was living with his family in a Chinese province – this was prior to the invasion of Tibet. A huge 'donation' was demanded by the Chinese before they would allow him to return to 'his' monastery in Tibet. That it was paid shows how important the reincarnation was. When the Chinese invaded Tibet and took over the country, the Dalai Lama was forced to flee.

His 'second in command', the Panchen Lama, has the task of confirming the new incarnation of the Dalai Lama after his death. So, when the Tenth Panchen Lama died a few years ago, it was extremely urgent that his new incarnation be found. The small boy was found in 1995 by agents of the Dalai Lama, and taken to a monastery in Tibet. Unfortunately, despite the Dalai Lama officially recognizing the new Panchen Lama, China has taken the young lama into 'protective custody' and tried to foist an impostor on Tibet by insisting that the Panchen Lama 'saw' his successor being found by the drawing of lots. (The Chinese had a candidate of their own.)

This is extremely significant for the continuance of Tibetan religion. If an 'impostor Lama', under the control of China, is in charge of the search for a new Dalai Lama then there is no assurance that the new Dalai Lama will actually be the reincarnation of the old. The centuries-old chain will be broken. China has, of course, a vested interest in ensuring that Tibetan Buddhism, and the line of the Dalai Lama, ends. Political expediency, or non-expediency, has historically been one of the reasons for belief in reincarnation dying out – people will die for their beliefs if they believe they will be reborn to a better life. (It

'READ IT'

The fourth approach to past lives entails 'reading' the past. A psychic or other sensitive person tunes into either the past life memories of the person concerned, or reads the Akashic Record which, it is believed, holds the epic tale of all of humanity's lives – and much else besides. This can produce some startling information, some of which is unknown at the time of the reading, but the proof can only be subjective at best. It is heightened if several psychics 'see' the same life. I once told someone about an obscure life in a remote part of the world in a period then more or less lost to history. "Oh yes," he said. "You are the third person to pick that up." Some years later, a television programme incidentally confirmed many of the salient facts whilst investigating an historical artefact.

I was reminded recently by one of my clients that I had told her of a life as a minor Egyptian prince, a son of Ramses II. Apparently I told her that her tomb would be found 'quite soon' and it would contain evidence of that life. She was most excited when the discovery was announced of a tomb containing many of the sons of Ramses (he had almost a hundred). As she has always believed in reincarnation, she did not need 'proof' but she is now awaiting confirmation of her previous existence with interest.

'EXPERIENCE IT'

The final approach is the one past life therapy takes: to relive the past in graphic detail with all the feelings and sensations of that life. This is what convinces most people. As someone said to me the other day, "I felt what it was like to be totally in love. It was overwhelming. I have never ever felt that in my present life, nor anything close to it. But now, I know that kind of love exists because I felt it then and I will recognize it when I meet it in this lifetime."

PAST LIVES: TRUE OR FALSE? DOES IT MATTER?

Unfortunately, one of the greatest arguments against past lives is the number of people who believe they have been someone famous (or infamous). It seems that when we begin to explore past lives, the same old faces come up again and again.

For instance, over the course of this century many people have been told, through channelled sources or their own regression, that they have been Mary, Joseph, even Jesus, one of the disciples, etc. Edgar Cayce often mentions his clients being 'at the foot of the cross' or 'in the Holy Land when the Saviour walked the earth'. Several people believe themselves to be Peter. I have always found it difficult to believe that such a short period in history, no matter how seminal, could contain quite so many souls in physical incarnation. Nonetheless, I have had four different clients who firmly believed that they were Judas, and the same regression has been reported from other therapists in the UK, Germany, Holland and the USA. I have also spoken to people who regressed to 'being Judas' but who refused to believe it was their own personal experience.

There are different explanations for this phenomenon and the

mere fact that it exists does not invalidate past life memories. Jung's collective unconscious is just one possible interpretation: at some very deep level we all share the same past which can be accessed in hypnosis or other altered states. Archetypes and 'classic scenarios' are another. It has been suggested that there are in total only a handful of stories which humankind is repeating over and over, each of which has an appropriate archetype attached to it. So, in the case of Judas there is a resonance with the betrayer.

It is theorized that we tune into the past life memories of all our soul group, that 'piece of spiritual essence' which broke off from the source way back in the beginning. In this way, each part of the soul group's experience raises the consciousness and completes the experience of the whole group without necessarily having had to undergo each life ourselves. Each soul group may well work through each of the 'classic scenarios' mentioned elsewhere.

Over-identification is yet another explanation. If someone has been strongly identified with a historical figure, such as Gandhi or a pop star like Jimi Hendrix, they make that experience their own. But they cannot know the fine detail, as do people who regress to these figures. Dolores Cannon, another highly experienced practitioner, is of the opinion that if you need an experience you have missed out on, you can get it 'imprinted' before incarnation. On the other hand, some people need to believe that they were important in the past to offset deep feelings of inferiority now, and wishful thinking cannot be underestimated. However, I believe something more important is happening in this shared regression, something to which I do not yet have an answer.

Archetypes

Potent, eternal and universal symbols that arise from the collective unconscious to illuminate our experiences. The archetypes cross cultural and racial boundaries. They are the common core experiences of all our lives.

What seems to be important is not that we should see past lives as 'fact' but that we should see them as telling the story of our soul's evolution and progress. Our 'past lives' then help us to understand our present situation, and teach us how we can grow in accordance with our soul's purpose. If we use reincarnation in this way it does not matter whether it is absolute fact or not, it is true for us on the inner levels. So, although for some believers in reincarnation, evidence matters, for others it is irrelevant. For disbelievers, lack of evidence is crucial. But for past life therapy to work, reincarnation does not have to be verifiable or literal, factual truth. Indeed, whilst I and all the therapists I know, believe in other lives, I think we would all say that not every regression is necessarily to an actual, factual past life. Nor does that matter. The test is whether they illumine and inform our present life. As Denys Kelsey points out, such experiences are a psychological reality if not actuality. In essence, these 'regressions' tell that person's story. If they are accepted as such and worked with therapeutically, then they have value.

THE HISTORY OF
PAST LIFE THERAPY

I f regression experience itself is to be believed, past life therapy is very ancient indeed. Several people 'remember' lives in the temples of Egypt working to help people overcome their past life traumas. Others have gone back still further in time, to Atlantis and beyond.

The 'soul retrieval' practices of Native American Indians (North and South) and other shamanic cultures stretch back into the distant past. The Tibetans too have karmic healing practices that go back at least 2,500 years – their particular version of Buddhist thought incorporates many of the practices of an earlier shamanic belief. Hypnosis is an old yogic tool. The Hindu sage Ramakrishna put his disciple Vivekananda into a trance when they first met so that Vivekananda could remember who he was before his present birth. His answer confirmed he was to be Ramakrishna's successor.

Modern western therapeutic approaches to past lives began with the rediscovery of hypnosis by Franz Anton Mesmer (1734–1815). But it needed the development of psychoanalytic techniques and the revival of ancient doctrines such as reincarnation embodied in Theosophy and other esoteric disciplines which occurred towards the end of the nineteenth and beginning of the twentieth century to really get the basis of past life therapy established. Madame Blavatsky, founder of Theosophy, and Annie Besant and Alice Bailey who incorporated many of her ideas, extensively developed the concepts of reincarnation and karma and their relevance to present life experiences. Their work was further expanded by occultist Dion Fortune. (Most modern day hypnotherapists would, however, be horrified by any suggestion that they were following an occult path.)

HYPNOSIS

Mesmer did not practise hypnosis as we know it or past life exploration, but in 1904 Lt Col Albert de Rochas hypnotized 19 people and took them back to past lives. At the same time, spontaneous past life memories were arising in pioneers of esoteric healing and in early psychoanalytic work. It was an idea whose time had come – but it developed slowly.

Towards the middle of the twentieth century, there was an explosion of interest; some of it reluctant. Many of the practitioners had been using hypnosis for some considerable time, up to forty years in some cases. In England, Dr Alexander Cannon, who was knighted for scientific achievement, regressed over a thousand people to other lives. He stated that "the majority of people do not benefit from psychoanalysis because the trauma lies not in this life but in a past life." In a typical Cannon case, a businessman who had a fear of going down in lifts regressed to being a Chinese general who fell to his death from a great height. In another case, a patient with an irrational fear of water died in chains as a galley slave who drowned at his post. However, Dr Cannon spent many years trying to disprove reincarnation, arguing with his patients that they were imagining it all. Eventually he had to give in to the overwhelming body of clinical experience he had amassed.

Early pioneers like Helen Wambach and Hazel M Denning published their work and nowadays many hypnotherapists use past lives, although there are some who still do not believe in them. Some of the best accounts of the therapeutic use of hypnosis in past life recall currently in print are to be found in psychiatrist Brian Weiss's books and in the work of the doyenne of American past life therapists, Winafred Blake Lucas.

THE PSYCHICS

Edgar Cayce is perhaps the best known past life practitioner of all time. In the course of his lifetime he gave over 15,000 psychic readings, not all of them pertaining to past lives although some 2,500 of them certainly did. In many cases, he never even saw the person he read for. He would simply have the name and location.

A relatively uneducated man from Hopkinsville, Kentucky, he nevertheless displayed an extraordinary knowledge of healing and philosophy. A fundamentalist Christian, he read the Bible every day of his life. This did not, however, prevent him from believing in other lives although he did say: "Life is for the doing today." Born in 1877, he was psychic from birth. As a child, he had a vision of an angel and asked that he may help others.

Cayce did his readings in a self-induced trance. He recognized that the cause of illness came from the mind and emotional frustration, rage and anger. His readings included very specific instructions for healing conditions. People had to be prepared to work hard if they consulted Cayce, but his 'cures' which included herbal preparations were usually effective. His abilities were revealed when he was himself hypnotized for loss of voice. The hypnotist suggested he should look in his body for the cause. He not only saw the cause, he also saw how

to cure it. Part of that cure entailed reading for other people. Whenever he tried to give up his spiritual work, his throat condition returned.

Up to 1923 he undertook physical and health readings for the people who came to him. Then he traced the past lives of Arthur Lanvers. Having been asked about the astrological chart, Cayce stated that more important than the urges from the planetary influences were the drives, talents and abilities which came to the man from previous lives on earth. Casually he said: "In the last incarnation, he [Lanvers] was a monk." Cayce didn't at first believe it, but Lanvers persuaded him that it was so. Cayce did 'life readings' for family and close friends. He gave names, dates and places as well as the talents and abilities they had in past lives. He also pinpointed relevant physical or psychological problems. From that time on, his readings often included past life information, especially the cause of present life disease.

Cayce himself was 'told' of many of his own past lives and they are an interesting illustration of the diversity of karmic experience. He believed himself to have been Pythagoras and several early spiritual teachers. However, the karmic problem that resulted in the enforced trance work seems to have started in ancient Egypt as a High Priest who had a 'weakness of the flesh' and broke his vow of celibacy when tempted by a priestess into making a 'perfect child'. It culminated in two lives as 'John Bainbridge', one in the 17th and the other in the 18th century. Both men were described as troubled, restless souls: 'wanderers and wastrels'. Each had a lustful disposition and irresponsible character with promiscuous relationships featuring strongly. The chain of incarnations was 'self-seeking in all respects', sexually, financially and morally. Cayce said that the reasons behind these lives was that he had to know the extremes in order to help others. At the end of the second John Bainbridge life, he gave his life in order to save another.

PRINCIPLES OF PAST LIFE THERAPY

Christine Hartley was another psychic who had the gift of 'far memory'. Again, she was psychic from birth. An ability that was not well received by her upper-class Victorian parents. Alan Richardson, another of Christine's pupils, has described her mother as "a jewel of Victorian narrowness, the sort who counted imagination as a vice to be suppressed". And yet, it was her mother who matter of factly told Christine, "Oh yes, it's quite common – your Aunt Augusta had it" after Christine had described a sense of déjà vu (which for years after was known to Christine as 'doing an Augusta'). Her father, a noted neurologist who studied the brain extensively, was convinced his child was, at the very least, suffering from delusions.

Christine did not, however, at first believe in reincarnation. She says she resisted strongly for many years. Then, one day she was cogitating on how a close friend of hers, someone 'so intrinsically good, so basically virtuous, not to say saint-like, though human enough to have made her mistakes in the past', be allowed to suffer great pain (having been abandoned by her husband and left to bring up three small children), while Christine herself at the time enjoyed excellent health and a very good life. She says it was like a great light dawning. Suddenly, she realized the only explanation was reincarnation.

In the 1930s Christine trained in the occult arts with Dion Fortune and Colonel CRF Seymour (known in her books as FPD). Her natural talents were honed. She was taught to 'read the records'. She would enter into an altered state of consciousness, withdrawing her awareness from the outside world, and access the Akashic Record. Christine was adamant that she was not in hypnotic trance, self-induced or otherwise. She had an abhorrence of hypnosis as she believed one should never willingly surrender one's will.

Christine occasionally 'saw' past lives spontaneously. Walking on Hadrian's Wall with her husband, she said, "Your name

was Marcellus and you were here throwing dice in that corner with three other men." Her scientifically trained, and somewhat pragmatic, husband merely said, "Was I? How interesting." On the whole, however, she would sit, either alone or as part of a group, and 'read the records'. Much of her reading was done to ascertain the past life causes of present life problems. She looked at the root of phobias and other conditions, and reconnected people to skills which they had once learned and required in the present life. Her own lifelong claustrophobia was traced back to an experience on the Nile. Christine was doing a joint 'seeing' with two other people but, up to this point, she had herself been able to see nothing:

"It was only as they described the boat coming to this point [the entrance to a temple] that I woke up, fully conscious. It was horrible. I was in the sarcophagus and the blackness and the sensation of fear were terrible. Dimly I heard FPD give a password at the door and it swung back and I knew that we were in a great hall filled with water and that I was still shut in on the barge. I could hardly control the agony that filled my mind … They took the lid off the coffin and then an inner shell and there I lay, with the blessed light on my face, my body bound round with grave clothes and no strength left in me. I was still dizzy from the drug I had been given to make me simulate death."

Unfortunately, no reframing was done. In Christine's own training, recall was deemed to be sufficient. In this case it was not. Although it improved to some extent, when I met her, some thirty or forty years later, she still could not bear to be in a confined space. She left instructions at the local hospital that she was not to be revived if brought in 'dead' – but nor was her coffin to be nailed down until they were absolutely sure she had finally and totally expired. She had a horror of being buried alive, not surprising after that Egyptian life when she had had to simulate death in order to escape being killed, but woke up too soon.

Some years later, however, we did manage to heal her equally lifelong fear of horses. We 'saw' her killed under the hooves of a stampeding horse. By this time she had trained me, and I had incorporated other elements into my work. We 'reframed' her experience and, at the age of 83, she was extremely proud of herself when she managed to walk through a field of horses for the first time ever.

THE MARRIAGE OF PSYCHIATRY AND PSYCHISM

Denys Kelsey, a practising psychiatrist, is a pioneer of past life therapy. He says he was precipitated into psychiatry in 1948 when he had to take over from the psychiatric duty officer during a flu epidemic in a military hospital. He learned that he had a talent for hypnosis at the same time when he 'accidentally' induced trance in a highly disturbed patient. During his early clinical days, he used hypnotic techniques with his patients. To his surprise, he found that the causes of present day problems often lay in other lives and he effected many 'cures'.

When he married the psychic Joan Grant in 1958, his therapy took on another dimension. Joan Grant had the ability not only to 'see' other lives, but to enter into them on behalf of someone else and to bring about changes. A powerful healer, she could 'take on' the conditions of her patients, drawing off the negative energies or diffusing traumatic situations. By the time she met Denys Kelsey, she had been doing this work for twenty years and had written several books about her own past life experiences. Having had spontaneous past life recall as a child, she trained herself in 'far memory' but her most powerful recall came from psychometrizing [psychically reading] a scarab which prompted 115 sessions dictating her own past life memories. This led to a 120,000 word book about Sekeeta, an Egyptian priestess trained in far memory work. Joan Grant would often sit in on sessions with Denys Kelsey's patients, discreetly directing the course the therapy took by writing her psychic impressions of past life causes on a pad which she would hand to her husband. He would then suggest his patient explore the relevant life. Between them, they effected some potent cures.

PSYCHOTHERAPY

Roger Woolger is probably one of the best known, and most innovative, past life therapists in both the UK and USA today. A Jungian analyst trained in Zurich, Roger too did not always believe in past lives – he still prefers to call them 'other lives' and has reservations about reincarnation in general.

Roger Woolger graduated from Oxford University in the mid-1960s with a degree in behavioral psychology. He says his mind had been put into 'a carefully tailored straitjacket'. A straitjacket from which it was partially liberated by years of meditation combined with membership of the Society for Psychical Research (whilst remaining sceptical), and by studying comparative religion at London University (although the concept of karma and reincarnation remained academic).

Then in the early 1970s he was asked to review Dr Arthur Guirdham's book *The Cathars and Reincarnation*. In this book, Dr Guirdham, a practising psychiatrist, recounts one of his patients' past life memories, and the effect it had on both his patient and himself. It did not convince Roger Woolger, however; he thought it was 'a reincarnational soap opera'.

Moving to the States, he began work as a psychotherapist. One of his colleagues suggested regression to a past life. Sceptical to the last, Roger agreed. To his surprise he found himself in a Cathar-period incarnation, but one that was nothing like the Guirdham book. He was a soldier, a "very crude peasant

turned mercenary", employed by the King of France to wipe out the heresy of Catharism. He found himself "in the thick of most hideous massacres in which the inhabitants of whole French cities were hacked to pieces and burnt in huge pyres in the name of the Church." He did not want to believe it. But it did explain aspects of dreams and fantasies that years of psychoanalysis had not touched. The end of that story explained a present life phobia: fear of fire. The mercenary had eventually "gone over to the enemy". He was caught and burnt as a heretic. As Roger says, aspects of that life were reflected in so much of his current life that he finally had to believe it. After that experience, he extensively studied and partook in regression work. He also read everything he could get his hands on regarding reincarnation and the various techniques available for accessing past lives.

Like so many others, Roger Woolger had no choice. He simply had to begin taking his clients into the realms of other lives, into what he calls 'unfinished dramas of the soul'. He says: "I have come to regard this technique as one of the most concentrated and powerful tools available to psychotherapy short of psychedelic drugs." But he also says he is still not sure of 'past lives' and reincarnation, but this does not matter because it is not necessary to believe in these things for past life therapy to be effective. He believes all healing comes from the power of the unconscious mind. In his therapeutic practise, he utilizes a "very precise cathartic working through" to "let go of and fully clear the trauma at all levels: physical, emotional and mental." In both personal therapy and workshops, he has now taken hundreds of people into other lives.

THE WAY AHEAD

Past life therapy is becoming more and more widely accepted. The idea of having had other lives which impinge on the present is being explored. Psychiatrists such as Dr Brian Weiss are continuing to stumble on the therapy 'accidentally' but are willing to tell the world what they have found. Pioneers like Dr Woolger and other highly experienced practitioners participate in the on-going training of therapists (see resource directory). It seems to be only a matter of time until conventional psychotherapy, and perhaps even psychiatry, broadens its horizons to encompass the idea of other lives impinging on the present. However, I remember Christine Hartley saying that back in 1973. In over twenty years we have advanced a little, but nowhere near as far as she envisaged. For every 'convert' to other lives, there is still a sceptic maintaining 'It can't be true.' To my mind, personal experience remains the most convincing reason for accepting the therapeutic value of regression, and perhaps this is how it should be.

HOW TO FIND
A THERAPIST

There are a great many past life therapists. So how do you select exactly the right one for you? Well, you can start by asking yourself what it is you are looking for. Is it merely curiosity about who and what you were? Or are you looking for something deeper? Not all the people who can take you back into past lives are willing or able to deal therapeutically with your experiences. If you identify what you expect of, and what you are seeking from, a therapist, this will help you to choose the best therapist for you. If you know the pitfalls, it will help you to avoid the wrong one. Knowing the right questions to ask will also help you to identify an appropriate therapist.

COST

Money may be an issue: "Can I afford it?", "Am I being overcharged?", "Why does one therapist charge so much more than another one?" are all questions that come up. Charges do vary, and it is not always the good therapists that charge the most: having made an appearance on TV can boost the fee by fifty or a hundred per cent, for instance. How much you spend should depend on the value you feel you receive. If you are taking good care of yourself, giving yourself what you need, then you will be willing to find the necessary money. Having said that, asking around will quickly establish a 'norm' and you can question whether higher charges really will give you better therapy.

'Cut-price' therapy is rarely of any value – which is why many therapists insist on therapy being paid for with money you have earned. Therapy then becomes an energy exchange. Some people question the ethics of charging. People whose primary aim is to help others, and who do this successfully, have every right to charge for their expertise accordingly. However, some people believe that being a therapist is a good way of making easy money. If making money is the primary aim of a therapist, then perhaps they are in the wrong job.

THE PITFALLS

Past life therapy is fast increasing in popularity. It is becoming trendy. Unfortunately, this can attract the wrong kind of person to the work. Such a person may be flamboyant, showy, skilled in marketing and self-promotion. He or she may soon become 'famous', a face or name you see everywhere. They are seen as 'experts', the media love them. But, they may not be genuinely interested in helping people improve their life: the aim of therapy. Nor may they necessarily know how to work therapeutically with past lives. Such people are easy to spot. They tend to have an 'I'm here to convince you/fix you' approach. They simply want to be 'a past life specialist', not therapist. (You could try asking who they were in a past life, the answer might be illuminating.)

On the other hand, there are people who 'jump on the bandwagon' in a different way. They may be hypnotherapists, bodyworkers, your Auntie Maud. They have the ability to induce extremely vivid past life recall. But this does not necessarily mean that they will know how to do past life therapy. Indeed, many of them back off as soon as a trauma surfaces, they simply do not know how to handle it and may actually create problems. So, beware!

As mentioned in the introduction, the training and registering of past life therapists does not come under a central body in either the United Kingdom or the United States. Nor, as far as I can ascertain, does it do so in other parts of the world. To a great extent, training depends on the willingness of a prospective therapist to take all necessary steps to be as competent as possible. Some organizations monitor their members and have a complaints procedure, others do not (very few of the organizations I contacted answered my questions on these points). In cases where certificates have been removed for malpractice or a breach of ethics, there is nothing to stop that person then setting up practice outside the umbrella of the association. Action can only be taken by the association against continued use of the qualification.

Membership of an association does not automatically guarantee that someone is competent to go deeply and therapeutically into past lives. Nor does a certificate guarantee that a 'therapist' will have had hands on experience. At least one hypnotherapy association in the UK hands out certificates to people who have done a postal course with no assessment of competence to practise on real people. So, a qualification or membership of an association does not always equal professionalism.

And, what is more, some of the best and most experienced therapists have had to learn as they go so they do not have a piece of paper saying that they can do past life therapy. Nevertheless, you may be much safer in their hands than with someone who has a multitude of framed certificates to practise ostentatiously displayed on the wall.

One of the pitfalls rarely mentioned, but often encountered in the 'public image' of past life work, is the desire to be someone special, famous, traceable. There are therapists who pander to clients' needs in this respect, and places that somehow trigger such 'memories' for individuals or groups. Historically, we remember only a handful of individuals who have stood out from the crowd over the course of several thousand years. So, the odds are you were one of the faceless millions who also lived but whose lives made no marks on history, and you will experience a past life accordingly. On the surface, these lives may appear mundane, unexciting. When explored, they explain so much of our present life experience. Nevertheless, there are people who seek out glory in a past life to compensate for their own feelings of inadequacy, or boredom, with their present life. They are not content with these seemingly mundane lives. If you are one of these people, you may well attract a therapist who aids you in your quest. Equally, there are therapists who always seem to trigger memories that are of being 'someone special'. Are such memories always true, or are they pandering to the ego of therapist and client? Such questions need to be addressed if you are to find a sense of authenticity in your therapeutic work.

So, although actually finding a suitable therapist may prove difficult, it is not impossible. There are some excellent people out there, you just have to do a little work to track them down.

> **Not all hypnotists are hypnotherapists.**
> **Not all hypnotherapists do past life work.**
> **Not all past life therapists are hypnotherapists.**

Sample Guidelines of Practice (College of Past Life Healing)

1 The basis of the work is one to one.
2 To keep confidentiality and provide a safe and sacred space for the client.
3 To honour the client's experience and not intrude our own agenda.
4 Not to abuse our position of trust for personal gain of any kind.
5 To honour the client's spiritual journey and their absolute connection with their own spiritual truth.
6 To empower the client to take responsibility for their own healing.
7 To undertake to continue with our own spiritual path.
8 To continue to work on our own issues.
9 To be totally present whilst working with our clients.
Plus: to make clear and simple boundaries: How much, how long, etc and to tell the truth fast, e.g. I can't help you any more.

Under no circumstances should a therapist suggest sexual contact with you. Nor should you have a relationship with your therapist whilst in therapy. This is highly unethical behaviour on the part of the therapist, and a most unwise course of action for you.

WHERE TO BEGIN

Approaches vary so widely in intention and practice that it is vital to find exactly the right therapist for your needs. You may have to be prepared to travel some distance, the person on your doorstep will not necessarily be the one you are seeking. Do not be afraid to 'interview' several therapists until you find one with whom you feel comfortable and whose aims match your own. If possible, meet face to face. Ask questions and do not be blinded by science, jargon or mumbo jumbo. If you do not understand, ask and ask again until it is perfectly clear.

What to Look For in a Therapist

Experience
Personal integrity
A willingness to go deeply and therapeutically into their own
  and your other lives
Open mindedness and flexibility
Someone you feel comfortable with and trust

Some therapists use a particular psychoanalytic approach. For many, past life work is an adjunct to their main focus. Roger Woolger, for instance, comes from a Jungian analytic and Eastern philosophical background. He also incorporates dynamic bodywork and psychodrama into his wide-ranging therapy work. Therapists trained by him (see Resources Directory) will also have that particular slant to their work, but may well incorporate other disciplines and skills according to their own background. You may find other therapists use Reichian, psychodynamic or psychosynthesis techniques, amongst many others. Some are trained in shamanic practice, soul retrieval, etc. Do not be afraid to ask what a particular approach entails.

You may also find that therapists come from a particular 'religious' background, Christian, Buddhist, Spiritualist, Native American, etc. In the States, much more so than in Britain, some Christian orientated churches embrace the concept of reincarnation and past lives. Others most emphatically do not. Inevitably the therapist's own religious or spiritual beliefs will affect the work they do, as will the regressee's own concepts. It is quite clear from regression work that if a client's belief system is such that they cannot accept that something is happening in a certain way for a certain reason, then they will shut it off, or try to explain it away. A belief system which stems from a closed mind may also hinder regression work.

I have an eclectic approach to my work, encompassing beliefs and concepts from many systems. I had to develop this flexible approach as whenever I thought, "That's it, I've sussed it," something would happen to turn things upside down again. My fundamental belief is in the eternal, spiritual nature of a human being. Beyond that, after over twenty years' experience of past life therapy and other life states, I can only say, "Who really knows?" I firmly believe there is much more to life, and death, than we can know from the perspective of earth, and inevitably this affects my work. In the same way, your own beliefs will affect what you experience during regression. What is more, any therapist's belief system will affect how their regression work is structured also.

So, before you even consider meeting a therapist, a little preparatory work will save a great deal of time.

The first step is to identify what you expect and need from the therapist.

QUESTIONS TO ASK YOURSELF

1 Do I simply want to explore other lives, maybe to convince myself of the validity of those lives?
2 Am I seeking evidence?
3 Have I had glimpses of another life that I want to follow up?
4 Am I lacking purpose in my present life?
5 Am I particularly drawn to a specific period in history?
6 Do I want to explore my previous relationships?

7 Is something getting in the way of my present relationship?

8 Is the answer to be found in the past?

9 Do I want to connect to an old skill or talent?

10 Do I have a specific problem such as health that I suspect may be related to a past life?

11 Will it need healing or reframing?

12 Does it relate to a specific part of my body?

13 Am I afraid of re-experiencing that life for myself?

14 Do I have a phobia?

15 Am I looking for a one-off session or an on-going course of treatment?

16 Am I a 'therapy junkie' endlessly going from one new treatment to another? (If so, you could be escaping into past lives rather than seeking treatment).

17 Do I need the practitioner to have a specific, perhaps spiritual, viewpoint on past lives?

18 Will I be disappointed if I turn out to be an ordinary person leading an exceedingly mundane and humble life?

HOW DOES THIS HELP?

It narrows the field and focuses you on what you really want.

Say you answer yes to question 1. A competent hypnotist who undertakes regression to past lives should be able to help you. Active imagination, guided imagery and the Christos technique could also take you back to an appropriate life. If you just want to put your toe in the water, far memory or a karmic reading could give you details of previous lives without you having to experience them for yourself. But, if you also answered yes to question 2, then you might like to consider that hypnosis tends to throw up more 'facts': dates, places, names, than some other techniques. Simply rerunning a life is probably all you need at this stage.

If you did answer yes to question 1, you might like to consider attending a past life workshop first. Many therapists run weekend workshops and healing festivals offer mini workshops to give you a taste. One or two day workshops give you an opportunity to explore several lives before going on to in-depth regression later if you wish.

If you answer yes to questions 3 and 5, then active imagination and guided imagery will point you in the right direction, as will hypnosis. You may like to choose a therapist who allows you to 'stay on the surface', observing rather than reliving. Again, rerunning the life is probably sufficient.

On the other hand, if you answer yes to questions 10, 11, 12 and 14, then you need a therapist who is not afraid to take you deeply into past lives and who knows the appropriate techniques for healing what you find there. For instance, you need a hypnotherapist not a hypnotist. In this case, you might well like to consider a regression therapist who is also skilled in bodywork to help you to release the energy blocks. If you answered yes to 13, then it is vital that you find a therapist whom you totally trust with no reservations. You will probably need a few 'practice run' sessions first before you are ready to approach the traumatic life or lives. Even then, if you still do not feel totally comfortable, it is not too late to change therapists.

If you said yes to questions 6, 7 and 8, be prepared for some surprises. Again it depends on what depth of insight you need, and how far you are prepared to go in healing any problems you find. Relationships can be dramatically improved by past life therapy, if you are prepared to work at it and to have forgiveness: for yourself and others. They can also be ruined if all you are going to do is blame the other person. A competent therapist will not only trace the patterns with you, but will also help you to change them where necessary.

Answering question 7 affirmatively gives you several options. You might want to go into hypnotherapy or past life healing. But the difficulty may also stem from 'unacceptable' feelings that you shut off, either early in your present life or in another. Soul retrieval could well help you here, as would bodywork and emotional release therapy.

Question 17 needs careful thought. If it is essential to you that the therapist shares your viewpoint, is that viewpoint restricting you in some way? Would you perhaps be better with someone of an open mind who could be open to everything that happens, rather than trying to run the life in 'acceptable channels' according to existing beliefs. Many therapists do have a religious perspective and you may need to question them to ensure that they can cope with something that would clash with their belief or viewpoint.

If you said yes to question 18, perhaps you should seriously reconsider your motives in seeking past life therapy. You might be much happier with a straight re-run induced by any competent hypnotherapist. On the other hand, you may be in for some surprises.

WHERE TO START LOOKING

Having decided what kind of approach you are looking for, you can begin enquiries. Keep a lookout for talks on past lives. Many local groups or organizations have these and most 'New Age' festivals or psychic fairs have speakers or mini-workshops on the subject. Past Life Conferences, advertised in specialist and 'New Age' magazines, will have several speakers (but do make sure they are experienced therapists rather than media experts). This gives you a chance to see a therapist in action before you commit yourself, and to hear about the latest developments in the field. Many 'New Age' centres also offer Past Life advertisements in the magazines listed in the Resource Guide.

Ask friends or acquaintances for recommendations. This is one of the most reliable ways to find a competent therapist. Often you don't even need to ask. It is strange how, as soon as you decide you need something, the universe responds by someone 'just happening to mention' exactly that subject. You often find that once one person has gone for regression, several people you know go. Check whether they all went to the same person or different therapists, and if so, why.

QUESTIONS TO ASK FRIENDS

How was it for you?

Did you get what you went for? What was that?

Did you feel free to explore whatever you needed or were
   you pressured to go in a particular direction?

Was it a straight rerun or was therapy involved?

Was it what you expected, more than you expected, were
   you disappointed?

Has it had any noticeable effect on your life?

Did you approach anyone else? If so, what put you off?

How many sessions did you need?

What did it cost?

Was it part of on-going therapy work?

But remember, regression will be different for everyone. Just because your friend experienced a deeply traumatic life, or merely skated on the surface of a 'lovely happy feeling', does not mean you will. Bear in mind also that we all respond to people in a different way: you will not necessarily feel comfortable with the therapist your friend thought 'wonderful'. You may also feel happier with a different kind of approach, some

people like a strongly directive therapist, others much looser guidance. Some want to experience the feelings deeply, others to gain insights. Check any points that are especially important to you.

If your friends cannot help, contact a therapy association for recommendations and local therapists. Appropriate addresses are given in the Resource Guide at the end of this book. All have either come out of my own personal contacts or are highly recommended by people whose judgement and professionalism I respect.

You will find advertisements for past life therapists in the resource directory of magazines, but do bear in mind that, just because someone advertises, it does not mean the magazine endorses them as competent therapists. Having selected a few possibilities, make some preliminary telephone enquiries and, having narrowed the field further, arrange an exploratory interview if you feel it would help (some therapists insist on this).

QUESTIONS TO ASK A PROSPECTIVE REGRESSION THERAPIST

How long have you been doing this work?

What is your background and training?

What is your approach?

Do you specialize in any particular area (phobias etc)?

Do you merely rerun a life or do you offer therapeutic options?

Do you combine past life therapy with any other therapy or bodywork?

Do you come from a particular psychotherapeutic, religious or spiritual viewpoint?

Would you be comfortable going deeply into a traumatic life with me?

Are you prepared to offer back up if necessary?

Do you encourage clients to explore the between life state?

Do you have a rigid, fixed time schedule or do you let sessions last as long as they need to?

How much do you charge?

How many sessions is it likely to take?

Do you offer a preliminary exploratory session or interview?

TALKING TO PROSPECTIVE THERAPISTS

Remember to clearly state the reason why you wish to undertake past life therapy. Practitioners need to know relevant details: the depth at which you wish to work, any phobias, chronic disease states, relationship problems, etc, so that they can help you find the right approach. If you feel you will need interim counselling and support, ask if this will be available. Ask all the practical questions: frequency of sessions, the duration, likely number required, etc, and don't be afraid to mention money: many therapists offer an introductory interview to discuss the therapy free of charge or at a reduced rate.

The length of a session is also important. In my experience, sessions have their own natural end. Sometimes it may be necessary to go on a little longer to bring things to a therapeutic conclusion. If a therapist has a fixed time schedule, then problems can occur. One woman reported going to a therapist who said, "Sorry dear, your time is up," at the moment that a knife went into her throat. The therapist did not even ask her to remove the knife before bringing her back into the present moment and sending her out of the door.

Only when you are certain that this is the right therapist for you should you make an appointment for regression. If you are not absolutely sure, it is unlikely that you will be able to relax enough to enter into a past life.

AND AFTERWARDS?

Having had the first regression, do not be disappointed if this seemed to be at a superficial level. As long as everything else feels right, you will no doubt go deeper the second time.

As with any therapy, be prepared to feel worse before you feel better. Ingrained patterns can take a while to change.

What's more, from my long experience, I can assure you that much happens on a level just beyond your awareness so you are not always consciously aware of the healing taking place within you. In time you will notice the difference.

9

SELF-CARE AND SELF-TREATMENT

CARING FOR YOURSELF DURING THERAPY

The best self-care you can give yourself is to find an experienced, empathetic therapist who will help you to explore your past and enhance your present, not impose an arbitrary framework on your experience. You will also allow yourself as many sessions and as much time as you need, supplementing it with other therapies or an overview such as karmic counselling if appropriate.

SELF-CARE

Find the right therapist for you.
Give yourself plenty of love, kindness and space. Be non-judgemental and non-self-critical. Find a loving support network and avoid people who make you feel 'bad'.
Retain your sense of humour and sense of perspective.

Most people feel absolutely fine during past life work. On the other hand, a handful of people don't. You may possibly need to take time off from the world. To create a space in which to assimilate the material and make the appropriate changes in your view of yourself. This may range from a day or so to a week or so. I know of someone whose response to her first, traumatic, return to childhood was to take to her bed for a couple of weeks. Her reaction was extreme, but right for her. At first she refused to see anyone, did not eat and slept a great deal. She went into a deep, deep depression. Later she was able to talk to a sympathetic friend about what she was experiencing, someone who simply accepted what she said but did not judge or react.

When her therapist later queried why she had not contacted her for help, she said, "I had to do it alone." That was what her childhood had taught her, and she graphically lived it out during those weeks in bed, retiring to her safe space like a wounded animal. But, at the same time she "thought I would die," the pain was so great. At that point, she was beyond therapy, she simply needed to be with that pain, to feel everything she had shut out as a child.

Then, over the weeks and months as her therapy progressed it became clear that this was a very old pattern indeed, one that went way back into other lives. Her fundamental core problem was separation from the divine part of herself. The religion on which she had relied as a small child in her present life had let her down, indeed had contributed to the pain. But so had religion in other lives. The turning point in her therapy came when she could make contact with the spiritual side of herself. Then, once again she needed to withdraw from the world. Only this time, it was to spend time reconnecting to that lost part of herself. To meditate and simply be with her real self. This time, when she re-emerged, she was transformed.

As with all therapies, past life therapy may possibly make you feel worse before you feel better. Especially if there is deep seated trauma working its way out. Allowing yourself to feel, getting the support you need, taking the time for you will all help. You don't need to do it alone, however. Reputable therapists will always provide the support you need.

A sense of humour definitely helps. If you can laugh at yourself and all the convoluted situations you put yourself through in the past, you will not get sucked down into the mire again. So much of the 'recall' is symbol and analogy that you cannot in any case be sure that really was 'you'. A sense of perspective is required, and a healthy dose of scepticism.

As some of the material which comes up during past life therapy can show the side of ourselves that we much prefer to keep hidden, being kind to yourself, forgiving yourself when necessary, is also important. As is suspending judgement and self-criticism. If you beat yourself up every time you 'do something terrible', have an unacceptable feeling or uncover what you deem to have been a mistake, you will set back the therapy and undo all the therapeutic work.

As other people also tend to judge us somewhat harshly, it is wise to contain the information you are gaining about your other lives, at least in the initial phase. Whilst your friends may be eager to hear about your experiences, a chance word or apparent criticism from them could precipitate you back into the old pattern. On the other hand, if you have a close, warm and empathetic friendship or relationship with someone who accepts and supports you no matter what, this can only enhance the therapeutic value of the work you are doing. To know that someone else loves us no matter what boosts our ability to love ourselves in our entirety, and that includes our more obnoxious past life selves (we all have them). When it comes down to the essence of the work we do on all our lives,

so often the fundamental healing is to forgive and love ourselves exactly as we are, and were. Offering ourselves this love and forgiveness is the best self-care there is.

SELF-TREATMENT

There are many 'do it yourself' tapes and workbooks on the market to help you to explore your past lives. Almost all cater to the 'curiosity' level, and few seem to recognize the dangers that can await the unwary traveller into these realms. Some offer ways of transforming past life material. But, it is our most traumatic lives that imprint themselves most strongly onto our etheric blueprint, they lie nearest to the surface in our present life. So it is not surprising that it is this traumatic material that often comes out when we listen to tapes or do past life exercises. A few tapes claim to be all you need to heal the past and change your present life. The tapes usually, but not necessarily, talk you both into and out of the regression experience. They sometimes, but not always, suggest therapeutic ways of healing the past should this be necessary.

Some writers have suggested that during exercises the subconscious mind, or the Higher Self, will only give us the memories we can cope with and will switch off others. From the experiences of many people who have contacted me after 'do it yourself' therapy, this is not necessarily so. And, what is more, as we shall see, if the safeguards fail, you have no other way out. Books are even worse places to get stuck, at least with a tape someone is trying to lead you out again. You have an external voice to follow. With a book, if you stop reading, there is nothing guiding you.

If you do have past life material that is bursting to get out, it may well take the first available opportunity, no matter how inopportune that may seem to you. Meditation, massage, complementary therapies of all kinds, yoga, music, places, people, have all been known to trigger spontaneous regression. So, if there is an urge to explore your past lives, even if it is just the vaguest curiosity, go to a proper therapist. Don't simply turn to

---

Self-Treatment

Don't! Leave it to the experts

---

the tape recorder or pick up a book.

Speaking as someone who underwent several spontaneous regressions to extremely traumatic other life situations and who has a long experience of accompanying people into some very strange places indeed, I cannot emphasize strongly enough how highly dangerous I think it is to explore your past lives without adequate guidance and especially without therapeutic help at hand. My spontaneous regressions were one of the ways I learnt my craft. It was not a way I would have chosen. I was fortunate that my connection to 'higher guidance' was strong enough to see me through. I was extremely thankful to meet Christine Hartley, who had been exploring other lives for over forty years. She took me on as a pupil and taught me all that she knew. Even then, there was more to learn. There still is.

One of the most graphic examples I can give you for not simply putting on a tape and drifting off to explore your past life is this:

"I put on the tape and lay on my bed. It took me on a journey and eventually into another life. Everything was going along fine until suddenly a tree fell on me. I was paralyzed, couldn't move. The pain was excruciating. I shouted and shouted for help until I was exhausted. No one came.

"Then I realized that somehow the end of the tape had come

and gone. I had no idea how to get back to my present life. I was trapped. I prayed and prayed for help. I managed to reverse the process I had gone through to get there. That brought me back into my bedroom. I opened my eyes.

"But, when I tried to move to my horror I was still paralyzed. My chest hurt and I could not feel my legs at all.

"I lay there for hours and hours. Daylight faded. I cried and cried, and could not wipe the tears away.

"Suddenly there was a knock on the door. I realized it was a friend with whom I was supposed to be going out for the evening. I tried to shout but nothing came out. The house was in darkness. Would she think I had simply forgotten and gone out?

"Fortunately she had a sixth sense that something was wrong. She came in through the back door and shouted for me. She came up into my bedroom and saw me there on the bed. I managed to indicate the tape recorder with my eyes.

"She ran the tape back and played the end. It made no difference. So she talked me through it step by step. I had to go back into that life and tell her what was happening. She told me to ask my guide to move the tree. But I was still paralyzed. She told me to leave that body behind, to let go of the sensations. To come back into my present life whole and healed. Gradually I was able let go and the feeling began to come back into my body. She massaged me and then brought me a cup of tea.

"I sobbed and sobbed as I told her how lonely and helpless I had felt stuck on the bed. It seemed like an eternity. I don't think I will ever forget that experience, it has scarred me for life."

If you do get 'stuck', the passage of time will probably bring you out of it … eventually. But, will you have done the necessary healing work? What will you have stirred up? You may have just touched the tip of the iceberg as it were. Your psyche might have tuned into what was going on in the rest of that life without it coming into your conscious awareness. You may well then proceed to live out the old patterns completely unconsciously:

"As I drove I found myself heading for the bridges on the motorway. I kept 'coming to' to find myself inches from death. The third time I pulled over, deeply shaken. Although I wasn't in the least depressed, on the contrary, I was elated, I suddenly realized I was trying to kill myself."

This was someone who had met another woman and felt totally, utterly, and inexplicably, in love: immediately. Realizing that it could be a past life connection, she "sat down and meditated on it" that evening.

"I was in this beautiful old house (rather like the place where we met). I was very much in love, very excited. My lover was coming back. He had been away a long time. We were to be married. That was all I could get at the time but I knew that my lover was this woman and that, in that life, she had been a man."

She thought no more about it, until she started heading for motorway bridges. Then she came to me. Gradually the story came out. The man had not turned up. She never knew what happened to him. She thought he had abandoned her. Eventually, she killed herself.

To heal the damage in the present life, I had to regress the other woman as well. She went straight back to that life, in which she had been a soldier called to fight for his country. He had been fighting in another country, was captured, probably as a spy, tried, and summarily hung over the battlements. The problem was, he had no idea what was going on as the trial was in a foreign language he could not understand. There was no way to let those at home know what had happened. It all happened so quickly.

A considerable amount of reframing was needed and it had

to be done while they were both back in that life. First of all, we had to get the soldier to write home and have the letter smuggled out so that she knew what had become of him – although we never did find out why he had been tried, the language problem could not be overcome. Then, after his death, we had him travel to meet her to say goodbye in 'a dream'. Later, in the between life state, they were reunited once more. There, we made sure that neither of them carried the residue over into the present life.

Some people do seem to have a gift for doing this kind of work on their own. They can not only get themselves in and out of tricky situations, but they can focus on the core thought or identify the reason why a life is important to them now. They are usually people who have already done a great deal of work on themselves, or who have worked with inner guidance for a long time. Nevertheless, even they can fall into yet another trap: delusion or egocentricity.

Experienced therapists can tell the difference between an 'imagined' past life and a 'real' one. We know the kind of lifescript that attracts: we've all met our share of Cleopatras, Egyptian pharaohs, ancient Atlanteans, etc. We may well be able to help you find out why you needed to experience that particular script. We can gently move you away from one that expresses what you most feared might happen to you, or bring you face to face with the real traumas that you have been skirting over for so long.

If you are doing it alone, you may well find yourself telling everyone, "Oh yes, I was Tutankhamun's tutor you know," or "I was Nelson, I saved England," or America, or wherever. Maybe you were, someone had to be. But maybe you were not, maybe you simply resonate to that at some level. As 'New Age Guru' David Icke found when he came out of a euphoric state and announced to the waiting world that he was "The Son of the God-

head, whatever that might mean", considerable embarrassment,
not to say public humiliation and ridicule, can follow on too
precipitous an announcement of your former glory. Maybe too
you will have missed the point of accessing that particular 'life'.
After all, we do not access these things merely by chance: they
are in essence part of 'our' story.

So, if you absolutely must satisfy your curiosity by self-
exploration, do be aware of the pitfalls. At the very least, tell
someone what you are doing. Preferably have them stand by,
just in case. Ideally, seek out experienced help.

PRINCIPLES OF PAST LIFE THERAPY

ABOUT THE AUTHOR

Judy Hall is one of England's most experienced past life therapists. A qualified counsellor and karmic astrologer, she has been practising past life therapy and karmic counselling for over twenty years. She was initially trained by Christine Hartley, who herself had over fifty years experience. A former past life counsellor at the College of Psychic Studies and a tutor with the Isle of Avalon Foundation, she has worked with hundreds of clients and conducts workshops in Past Life Exploration all over the world. Having identified a need for expert training, she now teaches therapists from many different backgrounds how to incorporate past life therapy into their work.

Judy is an experienced lecturer and writer. Her articles on past life therapy have appeared in magazines in the UK, USA, Germany and Australia, and she has appeared on television in the UK and USA to discuss past life experiences. She is the author of three books on astrology, one on psychic protection and two on the menopause.

RECOMMENDED READING

Bache, Christopher M *Lifecycles Reincarnation and the Web of Life* Paragon House, NY, 1994

Bernstein, Morey *The Search for Bridey Murphy* Doubleday, NY, 1989

Cerminara, Gina *Many Mansions: The Edgar Cayce Story on Reincarnation*, Signet

Cockell, Jenny *Yesterday's Children*, Piatkus, 1993

Cott, Jonathan *The Search for Omm Sety*, Century Hutchinson, 1987

Cranston, Sylvia (ed) *Reincarnation: The Phoenix Fire Mystery*

Cunningham, Janet *A Tribe Returned*

Glaskin, GM *A Door to Infinity: proving the Christos technique of mind travel* Prism Unity

Goldberg, Dr Bruce *Past Lives, Future Lives*

Grant, Joan, and Kelsey, Denys *Many Lifetimes* Ballantine Books, NY, 1987 (and other Joan Grant books)

Hall, Judy *The Karmic Journey* Arkana, 1990

Hall, Judy *The Astrology of a Prophet?* (available from the author)

Harrison, Peter and Mary *Children That Time Forgot*

Hartley, Christine *A Case for Reincarnation* John Hale

Hodgkinson, Liz *Reincarnation* Piatkus, 1990

Holbeche, Soozi *Journeys Through Time* Piatkus

Ingerman, Sandra *Soul Retrieval*

Iversen, Jeffrey *More Lives than One?* Warner, NY, 1976, Souvenir Press, London

Lenz, Frederick *Lifetimes: True Accounts of Reincarnation* Bobbs Merrill, USA, 1979

Lucas, Winafred Blake (ed) *Regression Therapy* Deep Forest Press, 1993

Moody, Dr Raymond *Coming Back* Bantam, 1990

Motoyama, Dr Hiroshi *Karma and Reincarnation* Piatkus, 1992

Raheem, Aminah *Soul Return* Asian Publishing, CA, 1991

Ring, Kenneth Heading *Toward Omega: In Search of the Meaning of the Near Death Experience* William Morrow, USA, 1984

Rocha, A and Jorde, K *A Child of Eternity* Piatkus

Stern, Jess *Soul Mates*

Stevenson, Dr Ian *Children Who Remember Past Lives* University Press of Virginia, 1987 (and several other books)

Weiss, Brian *Many Lives, Many Masters* and *Through Time into Healing* Simon and Schuster, NY, 1988, Piatkus

Whitton, Joel, and Fisher, Joe *Life Between Life* Doubleday, NY, 1986

Williston, Glen *Discovering Your Past Lives* HarperCollins

Woolger, Roger *Other Lives, Other Selves* Bantam, NY, 1988, HarperCollins

Some of the best books on reincarnation are now out of print but can be obtained from Reincarnation International (see resource guide).

RESOURCE GUIDE

PRACTITIONER TRAINING
Woolger Training Seminars
1208 Rt 212
Saugerties
NY 12477
USA

Woolger Training Seminars
Briarwood
Long Wittenham
Oxford OX14 4QW
England

The College of Past Life Healing (Diane Park)
c/o 118a Regents Park
London NW1 8XL
England
Telephone: 0171 586 0690

TAPED KARMIC READINGS, WORKSHOPS AND PRACITIONER TRAINING

Judy Hall
Gardens House
Wimborne St Giles
Dorset BH21 5N
England
(sae please)

PRACTITIONER LISTS

Association for Past Life Research and Therapy
PO Box 20151
Riverside
CA 92516
USA

Directory of Past Life Therapists and Regressionists
PO Box 26
London WC2H 9LP
England
Telephone: 0171 240 3956

HYPNOTHERAPY ASSOCIATIONS

Atkinson-Ball College of Hypnotherapy and Hypnohealing
and Corporation of Advanced Hypnotherapy
PO Box 70
Southport
PR9 8JX
England
Telephone: 01704 576285

Institute of Clinical Hypnosis
28 Tantallon Road
London SW12 8DG
England
Telephone: 0181 675 1598

WORKSHOPS

Soozie Holbeche
c/o 260 Kew Road
Kew Gardens
Richmond
Surrey TW9 3EQ
England
Tel: 0181 948 4156

Denise Linn
Suite No 120
1463 East Republican Street
Seattle
Washington 98112
USA
Tel: 2006 528 2465

Denise Linn
New Life Promotions
Arnica House
170 Camden Hill Road
London W8 7AS
England
Tel: 0171 938 3788

Denise Linn
New Life Promotions
Lock Bag 19
Pyrmont
NSW 2009
Australia
Tel: 61 2 552 6833

Dolores Cannon
PO Box 754
Huntsville
Arkansas 72740
USA
(sae please)

BODYWORK
The Shen Therapy Centre
26 Inverleith Row
Edinburgh EH3 5QH
Scotland
(Practitioner list for UK)

CENTRES
Association for Research and Enlightenment
(Edgar Cayce Foundation)
PO Box 595
Virginia Beach
VA 23451
USA

MAGAZINES

Reincarnation International
Phoenix Research Publications
PO Box 26
London WC2H 9LP

The Journal of Regression Therapy
APRT
PO Box 20151
Riverside
CA 92516
USA

FESTIVALS (WITH PAST LIFE WORKSHOPS)

Festival of Mind Body Spirit
New Life Designs
170 Campden Hill Road
London W8 7AJ
England

Healing Arts
New Life Designs
170 Campden Hill Road
London W8 7AJ
England

The Spiritual Mind and Body Festivals
The Secretary
5 Clough Mill
Slack Lane
Little Hadfield
Stockport SK12 5NL
England

Of further interest…

PRINCIPLES OF NLP

JOSEPH O'CONNOR AND IAN MCDERMOTT

Neuro-Linguistic Programming (NLP) is the psychology of excellence. It is based on the practical skills that are used by all good communicators to obtain excellent results. These skills are invaluable for personal and professional development. This introductory guide explains:

- what NLP is

- how to use it in your life personally, spiritually and professionally

- how to understand body language

- how to achieve excellence in everything that you do

Joseph O'Connor is a trainer, consultant and software designer. He is the author of the bestselling *Introducing NLP* and several other titles, including *Successful Selling with NLP* and *Training with NLP*.

Ian McDermott is a certified trainer with the Society of Neuro-Linguistic Programming. He is the Director of Training for International Teaching Seminars, the leading NLP training organization in the UK.

PRINCIPLES OF
THE ENNEAGRAM

KAREN WEBB

There is a growing fascination with the Enneagram – the ancient uncannily accurate model of personality types linking personality to spirit. Most people can recognize themselves as one of the nine archetypes. This introduction to the subject explains:

- the characteristics of the nine types

- how the system works

- ways of understanding your own personality

- how to discover your true potential and attain it

- ways to enhance your relationships

Karen Webb is an experienced Enneagram teacher, counsellor and workshop leader. She has introduced many people to the system and guided them in using the information to change their lives. She has been employed by many large companies as a management consultant.

PRINCIPLES OF HYPNOTHERAPY

VERA PEIFFER

Interest in hypnotherapy has grown rapidly over the last few years. Many people are realizing that it is an effective way to solve problems such as mental and emotional trauma, anxiety, depression, phobias and confidence problems, and eliminate unwanted habits such as smoking. This introductory guide explains:

- what hypnotherapy is

- how it works

- what its origins are

- what to expect when you go for treatment

- how to find a reputable hypnotherapist

Vera Peiffer is a leading authority on hypnotherapy. She is a psychologist in private practice in West London specializing in analytical hypnotherapy and a member of the Corporation of Advanced Hypnotherapy.

PRINCIPLES OF BUDDHISM

KULANANDA

More and more people are turning to Buddhism, disillusioned by the materialism of our times and attracted by the beauty and simplicity of this way of life. This introductory guide describes the growth of modern Buddhism and explains:

- who the Buddha was
- the ideas and beliefs at the heart of Buddhism
- how to meditate
- the main types of Buddhism in the world today

Kulananda has worked within the Friends of the Western Buddhist Order since 1975. Ordained in 1977, he is now a leading member of the Western Buddhist Order and, as a teacher, writer, speaker and organizer, is devoted to creating contexts in which Westerners can practise Buddhism.

PRINCIPLES OF PAGANISM

VIVIANNE CROWLEY

Interest in Paganism is steadily increasing and, while rooted in ancient tradition, it is a living religious movement. With its reverence for all creation, it reflects our current concern for the planet. This introductory guide explains:

- what Paganism is
- the different Pagan paths
- what Pagans do
- how to live as a Pagan

Vivianne Crowley is the author of the bestselling *Wicca: The Old Religion in the New Millennium*. She is a priestess, a teacher of the Pagan way and a leading figure in western Paganism. She has a doctorate in psychology and has trained in transpersonal therapy.

PRINCIPLES OF NUTRITIONAL THERAPY

LINDA LAZARIDES

Environmental pollutants and the use of antibiotics and other drugs cause changes in the body which can affect its ability to absorb and assimilate nutrients. Widespread nutritional deficiencies causing much chronic illness have resulted from this in our society. Nutritional therapists, complementary medicine practitioners working with special dies and vitamins, are often able to cure illnesses such as eczema, chronic fatigue, premenstrual syndrome, irritable bowel syndrome, hyperactivity and migraine.

This introductory guide explains:

- how deficiencies occur

- how nutritional therapy works

- which key illnesses the therapy can fight

Linda Lazarides is Director of the Society for the Promotion of Nutritional Therapy. She is a practising nutritional therapist with several years of working with a GP. She is an advisor to the Institute of Complementary Medicine and BACUP and is on the advisory panel of *Here's Health* magazine.

PRINCIPLES OF SELF-HEALING

DAVID LAWSON

In these high pressure times we are in need of ways of relaxing and gaining a sense of happiness and peace. There are many skills and techniques that we can master to bring healing and well-being to our minds and bodies.

This introductory guide includes:

- visualizations to encourage our natural healing process

- affirmations to guide and inspire

- ways of developing the latent power of the mind

- techniques for gaining a deeper understanding of yourself and others

David Lawson is a teacher, healer and writer. He has worked extensively with Louise Hay, author of *You Can Heal Your Life*, and runs workshops throughout the world. He is the author of several books on the subject, including *I See Myself in Perfect Health*, also published by Thorsons.